ONE ETERNAL WINTER

The Story of What Happened at Donner Pass, Winter of 1846-47

by

MARILYN W. SEGUIN

BRANDEN BOOKS
Boston

Library of Congress Cataloging-in-Publication Data

Seguin, Marilyn.
One eternal winter : the story of what happened at
Donner Pass, winter of 1846-7 \ by Marilyn W. Seguin.
p.cm.
Includes bibliographical references and index.
ISBN 0-8283-2060-8
1. Donner Party.
2. West (U.S.)--Description and travel.
3. Murphy, Virginia Reed, b. 1834?
I. Title.

F868.N5 S44 2001
978'.02--dc21 2001018495

BRANDEN BOOKS
Division of Branden Publishing Co.
PO Box 812094
Wellesley MA 02482

The remarks here made, in reference to the mildness and uniformity of the climate, are applicable only to the valleys and plains, for the mountains present but one eternal winter.

--from Lansford W. Hastings's Guide describing the routes to Oregon and to California

CONTENTS

ACKNOWLEDGEMENTS

I am grateful to my friend and Kent State University colleague Dr. Tom Davis, professor emeritus, for his encouragement and advice on this project from the very beginning. Dr. Davis provided research guidance as well as a careful reading of an early draft of the book. His suggestions and guidance have been valuable motivators. Thanks also to my friend Jane Ann Turzillo, photographer and writer, for her assistance. Jane traveled with me to visit the Sierra Nevada during the early stages of this project and served as a critical reader of the final manuscript.

Once again, I'd like to thank my family--husband Rollie, son Scott, and daughter Kathryn--for their continued support of my research and writing projects. Any mistakes are absolutely my own.

Donner Party Route

PREFACE

What happened at Donner Pass during the awful winter of 1846-47 has always been controversial to many, misunderstood by most. This is a novel about that incident, told from the perspective of one of the survivors, Virginia Reed, who was only twelve years old when she set out for California. Like any historical novel, this book is, in part, speculation. However, the characters in this story all existed, and most of the incidents described in these pages can be documented in the diaries, letters and memoirs penned by these people, including Virginia.

The setting is another major character of this story. Donner Pass is a rocky opening in the Sierra Nevada Mountain Range on the Nevada-California border. Sierra Nevada means "snowy range." Before emigrants pushed into the region, Native Americans warned early explorers of the dangers of getting trapped by deep snows. They described these mountains as "rock upon rock, snow upon snow."

Even today, the Sierra Nevada landscape is brutal and the weather is unpredictable. Indeed, when I first visited the Donner Pass area in 1999, I got caught in blinding snow and sleet as I ascended the mountains in my rental car on modern Interstate Highway 80. It was June 3. When the group of emigrants that came to be known as "the Donner Party" became trapped by the snows in the Sierra Nevada, they found themselves without adequate shelter or food. Those who survived did so for a number of reasons, including the loving care of their family members, their hope and faith that they would be rescued, and their resourcefulness in the face of deprivation. The events that occurred at Donner Pass in the winter of 1846-47 have been described as "a horrendous act against nature and against God" as well as "a testament to human courage and resiliency in the face of extreme circumstances." Human response to extreme deprivation varied depending on the individual's character. As Virginia Reed found out, a person's character in good times is not necessarily a predictor of how that person will behave in survival circumstances. Cannibalism was only an issue for a few of the survivors--and it played no part at all in Virginia's survival.

The Donner Party numbered 90 souls in all; 47 survived and 43 died. Eighty-one were trapped in the mountains during one eternal winter.

Marilyn W. Seguin
Gray, Maine
August 2000

PROLOGUE

December 1900

Dear granddaughter,

You have asked me to relate to you the circumstances of my long ago journey. The day we set out for California was one of the most exciting days of my life. I believed myself to be the luckiest girl alive, and I was smug with anticipation and joy. I could not imagine then that what happened later could ever happen. Now, thinking back on it, I wonder why it took me so long to realize what was happening on the shores of Donner Lake.

In my adolescent years, I adored my father. I thought him the most handsome, brilliant, exciting man on the face of the earth. Everything he did and every word he spoke reflected infinite wisdom and courage to my young mind. My father was impetuous and daring as any dime novel hero. In contrast, my mother was delicate, frail in her physical stamina, slow to speak her mind, reticent and demure in her demeanor as a proper lady was expected to be in her day. Early in life, I became aware that my beautiful mother often used her "sick headaches" as an excuse to withdraw from any unpleasantness. During those times, my mother would retreat to her room with the curtains drawn against the light which she said intensified her pain. My father had hired our maid and cook Eliza to help out especially in those times when my mother could not care for me and my younger brothers and sister. I thought my mother as weak as my father was strong. I had yet to learn that one's outward appearance or superficial behavior is not necessarily a gauge of the character beneath.

Most of those who later wrote about the group of us who came to be known as the ill- fated Donner Party regarded our actions as ghoulish and disgusting. In fact, no pen can describe the horror of it. One writer once asked me what it felt like to be so hungry I could eat my own dog. I couldn't answer him. How do you describe the color red to someone who is blind? Since then, I have never been able to enjoy a feast. Even a meal with more than one kind of food is too rich for me. Meat and potatoes? Not for me. Meat or potatoes. Christmas and Thanksgiving are especially difficult because of the abundance of food.

After I die, I ask that my body be burned and my ashes scattered over the plains where they will mingle with the fodder of the buffalo and wild ponies and I will become a part of them, for I have lived long enough to understand the vagaries of sustenance.

Your devoted grandmother,
Virginia Reed Murphy

PART I
The Great Adventure

I never could have believed we could have traveled so far with so little difficulty. Indeed, if I do not experience something far worse than I have yet done I shall say the trouble is all in getting started.

Tamsen Donner (in a letter written in June 1846).

CHAPTER 1
Looking West

Virginia Reed and her sister Patty sat atop Virginia's pony, Billy, and watched the road for signs of riders ahead. Beside them, their pet terrier, Cash, sat and whined, wanting to be off racing across the meadow that was part of the Reed family property in Springfield, Illinois. A weak, late winter sun warmed their faces as the girls gazed eastward, watching for some movement on the road ahead. It was late February, and although the grass was brown and brittle on the meadow, the snow had long ago melted, and spring was on its way.

"Pa said Uncle George and Uncle Jacob should be here this morning," said twelve year old Virginia to Patty, who sat behind her on Billy, clasping her waist tightly. Patty was only eight, but Virginia thought Patty acted more like, well, someone Ma's age, old and serious. Virginia preferred racing across the fields on her pony, while Patty was content to sit inside all day, playing with her dolls or talking to Grandma Keyes who was bedridden with consumption.

"Wise beyond her years," Ma said once about Patty.

"But she doesn't know how to have much fun," Virginia had complained.

"And you, young lady, don't know how to be serious," said Ma.

It was Ma who suggested that Virginia take Patty with her this morning to meet their expected guests. The Donner brothers, George and Jacob, weren't really their uncles, but Virginia and Patty and their younger brothers, Jim and Tommy, thought of them as blood relatives. James Frazier Reed, Virginia's father, had been friends with the Donner brothers for as long as she could remember. Today the Donner brothers were coming to visit with the Reeds to finalize their travel plans to move to California.

"Wait'll they get a look at our pioneer palace car," said Virginia. She couldn't wait to see the look on their faces when they saw the two-storey covered wagon that the Reed family would live in as they traveled west. Pa had designed his family's wagon to be as fine as the furniture he designed and built for folks in Springfield. The Reed wagon had doors on the sides that one entered by using a set of portable steps. A wood stove would heat the inside, and a chimney poked up through the canvas roof, prevented from setting fire to the roof by a circle of tin. The seats were on springs for comfortable riding, with storage underneath for medicines and bandages, and there was even room for books! At night the family would sleep on beds built into a loft, except for Grandma Keyes who would sleep on her own feather bed on the floor of the wagon. Although she was ill, Grandma Keyes, at age seventy, refused to be separated from Ma, her only daughter. Grandma Keyes was determined to go with them on the trip to California.

The pioneer palace car, as Virginia called it, would be their new home until they reached California the following autumn. But Pa and Virginia would not be riding in the palace car as they made their overland journey.

"You and I will ride horseback, Virginia," Pa had told her last winter when he laid out his plans before the family. And that was when Pa had given her Billy, a perfect little beauty of a pony, cream colored, with a heavy, dark mane and tail. Virginia had screeched with delight and thrown her arms around her father, thanking him over and over until he had to pry her loose. Cash had raced around them in a frenzy, but Billy gazed calmly at them all as if he knew that he was worth all the fuss.

Virginia on Billy and Pa on his racing horse, Glaucus, wouldn't be the only people in their group riding horseback from Springfield to Independence, Missouri. The Donners had hired teamsters to drive their wagons so the Donner brothers would be free to travel on horseback as well. Virginia looked upon the upcoming journey as one grand adventure. She could hardly wait!

Pa had hired his long-time sawmill employee Milt Elliott to drive his ox team. And the young, perky Eliza Williams, who helped Ma cook and take care of the younger children, had asked to go with the Reed family.

"I've an itching to see California--maybe even get married there. I can help Mrs. Reed on the trail the same as I do in Springfield," Eliza said. Pa had said that she could join them. Virginia was delighted.

"People will think that we're putting on airs, taking servants on the trail to do our work for us. And that wagon, that pioneer palace car, it's pretentious," said Ma one night at dinner. Virginia didn't know what "pretentious" meant, but she could tell by Ma's voice that it wasn't a good thing.

"I won't have any unnecessary hardship on this trip, Margaret. We can afford the help, and we'll need Milt and Eliza once we reach California. Let people think what they will," said Pa. Virginia knew that Pa was just looking out for Ma and wanted her to be comfortable, for Ma was a real lady who spent her days reading and playing the piano and doing fine embroidery. Pa would do anything for Ma, and although Ma loved him back just as much, she hadn't wanted to sell all their belongings in Illinois and move to a place she had never seen.

"But our friends, my brothers, your business, James. All that we love, all that we've worked for so hard all these years is here in Springfield. What is there for us in California?" Ma had said when Pa first suggested the idea. That had been after the Donner brothers had visited them last fall.

"There's land, Margaret. We're well off here in Springfield, but in California, we'll be rich! Think of it. It will be better for the children, better for all of us. And I hear the Sacramento Valley is warm and green and the weather is pleasant the year round. Such a climate could cure your sick headaches."

"And the Donners--what of them?" Ma had asked him. Uncle Jacob and Uncle George were both old men who had young wives. Between them, the two Donner families had twelve youngsters in their care. Uncle George had already moved five times before settling in Springfield. Now he wanted to move again.

"Tamsen and Elizabeth will go, and all the children too, of course," Pa said.

"*Will* go--not *want* to go?" Ma asked. She knew that Tamsen, especially, was gloomy about the idea of pulling up roots and heading west.

Still, as much as Ma resisted the move, Virginia had heard Ma defending Pa when Virginia's Uncle Gersham had called Pa a "malcontent," whatever that was.

"Some people are always drawn by a vision of things, a way of life that can be better. James is one of those people, I suppose. A malcontent? No, I'd rather call him a discontent," said Ma to Uncle Gersham. After that conversation, Ma took ill with one of her sick headaches, which could last up to a week. During those times Ma stayed in her room, in bed with the curtains drawn, and Patty and Virginia took her meals to her on a tray just as they always took Grandma Keyes her meals.

Virginia knew that she, Virginia, was the only one of the Reeds besides Pa who was truly excited about this trip. Even young Patty had been against the trip in the beginning.

"What about Cash and Barney?" Patty had asked her father. Patty loved the family dogs, especially the perky little terrier Cash. But Pa had reassured Patty.

"Cash and Barney will go with us. Barney is big enough to walk beside the wagons, but little Cash can ride inside with you, Patty."

And then Barney had surprised them with a litter of pups. Patty named the tiny hounds Trailer, Tracker and Tyler.

Patty tearfully declared that she would not go to California without the pups. Pa had relented.

"Well, seeing as the pups will be pretty big by the time we leave in April, I guess they can come along. But once we reach California, we'll have to find good homes for those pups. Five dogs is three dogs too many," Pa said. And Patty agreed, but Ma worried over taking so many dogs.

"How will we feed five dogs on the trail? Goodness, James, we've already got nine people to feed every day," said Ma.

"You leave that worry to me, Margaret. We'll carry much of our food with us in the supply wagon and hunt for fresh meat along the way."

Now, waiting for the Donner brothers to ride up the road, Virginia smiled in anticipation. All the things that mattered the most--her family and friends, Billy, the dogs-- would be with her on the great adventure of the trip to California.

As if he were reading her thoughts, suddenly Cash began barking and rushing madly around Billy, looking up at Patty for permission to run ahead.

Virginia squinted into the sun. She could see the Donner brothers on horseback just cresting the hill, and she urged Billy into a gallop up the road to meet them.

CHAPTER 2
Saying Goodbye

Pa and the Donner brothers stayed up late into the night, making the final plans for the trip. Virginia and Patty lay awake in their beds listening to the men talk. Each family would take three wagons--one to ride and live in like the Reed's pioneer palace car, one to carry food and supplies, and one to carry along furniture and equipment they would need once they reached California. The men consulted a book called *The Emigrants' Guide to Oregon and California* by Lansford W. Hastings, as they traced out their route.

"Hastings suggests a shortcut route through these mountains here," said Pa, tracing his finger along a map route.

"Leaving in April, that should get us to the Sacramento Valley by fall. Got to get over the Sierra Nevada before winter sets in," said Jacob Donner.

Virginia had never seen a mountain, but she imagined high rocky places covered with grass and flowers with snow covering the highest peaks in the winter. Mountains would be something to reckon with for the oxen pulling the wagons, she supposed, but she and Billy ought to have great romps in these high places. Virginia drifted off to sleep that night and dreamed of riding over the mountains covered with soft, fluffy white snow.

The next morning the Donner brothers left the Reeds, with promises to return to Springfield on April 15 with their families and wagons filled with all they would take with them to California. From Springfield, they would journey to Independence, Missouri, where they would join other families on their way to California.

In the final weeks before the departure, Virginia and Patty helped their mother and Eliza with the preparations. Even five-year old Jim and three-year-old Tommy helped carry the supplies to the wagons, where Pa found a place for each item-- flour, sugar, salt, bacon, coffee--in amounts large enough, according to the Hastings guide, to feed them until they reached California.

Even with three wagons, the family couldn't take all their possessions with them. Much had to be given away or left behind. Patty, who spent most of her time indoors playing with her dolls or talking to Grandma Keyes, agonized over which of her baby dolls to adopt out and which to emigrate to California. Virginia helped her father load the wagons.

"Will there be places to shop if we run low on supplies, Pa?" Virginia asked.

"There are a few trading posts at the forts. We'll also be able to trade for some things with the Indians, but mostly we have to carry what we need," he said. Pa showed her some colored beads and bolts of cloth and other things for trading with the Indians.

Of all the things they might encounter on the great adventure, Virginia feared only the Indians. Why Lansford Hastings himself, the author of the guide the Reeds and Donners used to plan their trip west, was once taken prisoner by the Indians on his way to California. What was to keep Virginia or Patty or their little brothers or any of them from being taken, or worse, tomahawked to death? In the long winter evenings in Springfield, Virginia and Patty begged Grandma Keyes to tell them stories about Grandma Keyes' aunt who had once been captured by the Delaware tribe.

"Indians in Kentucky where my aunt lived used to attack the cabins in the middle of the night. Clubbed some of the adults over the head with a tomahawk and took others, including my Aunt Mary, back to their villages to be slaves," said Grandma Keyes.

Virginia and Patty had sat on the floor in Grandma Keyes' room, their backs against the wall so no warrior with a tomahawk could slip up behind them. In the flickering firelight, Grandma's bedposts, even the shovel and tongs in the chimney corner, took on the appearance of savage Indians in feathers and paint, ready to swoop down on the girls and carry them away to a remote Indian village.

"What happened to your Aunt Mary, Grandma?" asked Patty, who knew very well what happened because she had heard the story dozens of times.

"Five years later, her brother came to the village to rescue her. She went back to her parents but she was never the same," said Grandma Keyes. "She couldn't ever sleep in a bed again. She slept on buffalo skins laid out on the floor. Wouldn't ever wear shoes, either. Went barefoot mostly, till the day she died."

Later, when Virginia had asked her mother if the Indians on the plains might kidnap her or Patty or one of her brothers, Ma had said probably not.

"More likely that they'd take the things that they can't get on their own--blankets, pans, clothing--they have children of their own, I suppose. Grandma Keyes shouldn't be telling such tales," Ma said.

Just in case Ma was wrong about what the Indians wanted, Virginia made sure that the things her father had bought to trade with them were packed close to the supply wagon entrance, so that Pa could get them in a hurry should he need to ransom any of their family.

The Reed women had a whole new wardrobe made for them to wear on the journey. Even Eliza would have new clothes, thanks to Pa's generosity. Virginia and Patty gave away some of their frillier dresses, but the plainer cotton dresses they had packed in strong canvas bags to take to California. On the trail they would wear dresses made of plain linen, with long sleeves and high necks to keep the sun from burning their skin. Virginia called the clothes their plains uniforms.

A week before their departure, their new clothes were ready for the final fittings.

Ma, who was accustomed to wearing silk dresses with low necklines and sleeves adorned with ribbons and lace, looked skeptically at the scratchy linen frocks. "Well, they aren't very pretty but we'll all need serviceable clothing for the trip," Ma said, "and the long sleeves will protect us from insects and dust."

Eliza whispered to Virginia. "I hear tell in the dry places on the plains, the rivers are so dry that steamboat passengers can't see the banks for clouds of dust raised by the paddle wheels," said Eliza. Virginia had seen plenty of steamboats, but she could not imagine paddle wheels churning through the dust.

When it was their turn to be fitted, Virginia and Patty giggled at their images in the mirror as the dressmaker pinned up their skirts.

"We'll all be glad of these clothes once we start to travel, I'm sure, and the linen will keep us warm in the cool weather," Ma said reasonably.

"Cool weather indeed! I hear tell that chickens hatched in the dry heat of the plains come out of their shells already cooked, Mrs. Reed. We'd best pack a few of our light summer dresses in case our plains uniforms get too hot," said Eliza. Virginia giggled. Sometimes Eliza made up such fantastic stories it was hard to know whether to believe anything she said. Virginia was glad the good-natured Eliza was coming with the family on this trip. Eliza could make even the always serious Patty smile when Eliza told her funny stories.

The day before they were to leave, Virginia and Patty helped Ma to sew tiny pockets into an old patchwork quilt. Into each pocket, they inserted a money piece and carefully stitched the pocket closed.

"Just in case we encounter any thieves on our journey. No one would ever think to look inside a quilt for money," explained Ma. Virginia thought it a clever idea. That evening, Patty asked Virginia to help her sew tiny pockets into the apron of her plains uniform so that Patty might have a hiding place for the things she decided to take with her. Patty called it her pocket skirt.

On April 15, the Donner wagons arrived in Springfield: George and Tamsen Donner with their five children, and Jacob and Elizabeth Donner with seven youngsters. The Reeds were ready, and nothing remained to be done except to say goodbye to their friends and neighbors. Ma's brothers were on hand, trying one last time to persuade their mother, Grandma Keyes, to stay in Springfield.

"I want to see the west, boys, and I won't leave Margaret," said Grandma Keyes stubbornly. Virginia's uncles would accompany the wagon train on horseback for several days and nights before saying their final goodbyes to the family and returning to their homes in Springfield.

Mrs. Lincoln, the wife of Pa's lawyer friend Abe Lincoln, came to wish them well.

"My husband is away from Springfield on circuit tour, or he'd have come to wish you good bye himself," said Mrs. Lincoln. Pa had served in the Black Hawk Campaign with Mr. Lincoln. Now Pa hoped that Mr. Lincoln's connections in California might help him find a job when the family reached there in the fall. He told Mrs. Lincoln that he would write to them as soon as he reached California.

Finally, all the goodbyes were said. Even Virginia's and Patty's schoolmates had come to say farewell, which made the Reed sisters feel very important indeed. Now it was time to leave.

Pa and Virginia's uncles carried Grandma Keyes out to the pioneer palace car and placed her on the soft feather bed. Patty sat on the end of the bed with Cash and held open the wagon cover so that Grandma Keyes could see her old home and say goodbye to the friends who came to wish them well on the trail.

Ma, who had been so busy and brave in the days leading up to the departure, was now overcome with sadness at leaving her friends and house behind. She sobbed as Pa led her from the porch of their house and helped her into the wagon. Virginia felt sorry that her mother didn't feel any of the excitement that Virginia felt. Many friends had decided to accompany the Donners and Reeds on the journey for the first day and spend the night in camp before leaving them in the morning. Tonight there would be eating and laughing around the campfire. To Virginia, the leave taking was a festive party and promised to be the start of a long pleasure trip.

Finally, the passengers were loaded into the wagons and the teamsters were ready, standing beside the ox teams that they would lead on foot 2500 miles from Illinois to California. Virginia mounted Billy and they stood near Pa who was astride Glaucus. Barney and her offspring were barking excitedly and racing around the wagons as everyone waited for the signal to be underway.

Virginia leaned over Billy and whispered in his ear, "Here we go, Billy. Carry me safely to California, where the sky is blue and the grass is green, and we can run across the fields every day, even in the winter."

Beside her, the Reed teamster Milt Elliott raised his whip and called, "All aboard for California!" Full of hope and courage, the emigrants began to move forward.

CHAPTER 3
Fun on the Trail

Virginia knew that sometimes you could build things up in your mind so much that the reality of it was just a disappointment. But nothing happened to dampen her expectations of the first days of the journey west. It was as she had built it up in her mind, day after sunny day of galloping across the fields on Billy with Pa and Glaucus, or sometimes leading Billy at a walk beside the pioneer palace car as Milt drove the oxen. Virginia soon discovered that Milt with his "whoa," "haw," and "gee" could make the oxen do whatever he wished, even though the oxen had no bridles.

On the trail, the families settled into a routine. In the mornings, Virginia helped Eliza prepare the family breakfast of mush or grits and bacon. During the day, while the wagon caravan moved slowly forward, there was nothing for her to do except ride Billy and enjoy the changing landscape. Ma and Patty and the boys sat with Grandma Keyes inside the pioneer palace car, reading and chatting and tossing the ball to little Cash who, unlike Barney and her brood, much preferred the safety of the wagon to the dangers of the oxen's feet.

Sometimes the Reed and Donner children spent the evening hours throwing sticks to the dogs or playing tag. At night the women baked bread in pans nestled in the coals of the campfire as they gathered together to tell stories and sing songs. After the bread was baked, the children slathered the hot bread with butter that Eliza churned during the day as she rode in the wagon.

"Hardly any work at all to churn butter on the trail," said Eliza with a wink. "Just set the churn in the middle of the wagon and the jolt of the ride churns the cream. By the end of the day, we've got butter!"

As Springfield slipped behind them during the warm days of April and early May, even Ma's spirits picked up and Grandma Keyes' health seemed to improve. The weather was fine and the company was in good spirits. Each day brought new delights as the landscape unfolded.

One day as Virginia rode Billy, she found an infant calf beside the trail. Its mother, one of the Reeds' cattle brought along in the herd that was part of the family's food supply, calmly grazed beside her calf, unconcerned that her newborn appeared to be dead. Virginia jumped off Billy and held the infant against her chest and rubbed the tiny body until the calf began to breathe. Then she set it gently beside its mother and laughed when the calf stood up unsteadily on wobbly legs and began to nurse, first gently and then more strongly, looking at Virginia as if Virginia, not its own mother, had infused it with the will to live.

On the day they reached Independence, Missouri, after two days of thunderstorms and downpour, they found the town's muddy streets crowded with other emigrants, people like themselves who were heading west to start new lives in California or Oregon. In Independence the emigrants bought supplies that would allow them to make the journey, for the town was one of the last outposts of civilization at which to shop. Virginia rode Billy around the fields outside of town, examining the wagons and equipment of the other travelers, and she pronounced the Reed's pioneer palace car equal or better than anyone else's wagon.

When they left Independence a few days later, many other emigrants with their wagons had joined with the Reeds and Donners. The travelers held a meeting and elected James Reed as their leader.

"The more wagons, the safer we are," said Pa, who had learned in Independence that a war with Mexico was heating up. But there was another reason for joining up with the other wagons, Virginia learned as she listened to the adults talking around the campfire that evening.

"Jacob heard that the Sioux are on the warpath up in Wyoming territory," said Tamsen Donner.

"Then all the more reason for us to welcome our fellow travellers," said Ma. "There's strength in large numbers. The Indians will leave us alone if they see that we are many."

That night, Virginia dreamed that an Indian on horseback chased her as she rode Billy over the plains. The dark-skinned warrior overtook her and Billy and raised his tomahawk, ready to strike. Virginia awoke, shaking in the darkness of the wagon.

The next day, they left Missouri and headed into Kansas. Still more wagons joined them on the way. As the weather stayed nice, Virginia resumed her wild rides across the fields as the wagons moved west. Sometimes in the mornings, she and Pa would ride far ahead of the slow moving wagons to scout out suitable ground for camp that evening. Then they would ride back again, sometimes stopping to rest and pick wild flowers to give to Grandma Keyes.

In mid-May they reached the Caw River. "The river is named for the Indians of this region," Pa explained. And Virginia was appalled when she learned that they must rely on these Indians to ferry them across the river.

Virginia sat atop Billy on the river bank and watched as the first of the emigrant wagons was loaded onto the raft that would carry it across the wide Caw River. She pulled out her spyglass so that she could get a closer look at the dreaded Indians. Her spyglass had been a gift from her cousin Mary who thought it might become useful for "scanning the plains." The spyglass was shaped like a cone and it collapsed to half its length for storage in its leather pouch. Virginia had assured Mary that the gadget would indeed be most useful for scouting buffalo and Indians, and she intended to do that now. When Virginia closed her left eye and looked through the spyglass lens with her right eye, whatever she was looking at appeared much larger than it would just by looking at it without the spyglass.

Now Virginia studied the Indians through her spyglass. The Indian men were shirtless, but otherwise were dressed just like the emigrant men--in cloth pants. Their skin was dark, and some of them wore feathers in their long black hair, but they were not painted on their faces and bodies as she had imagined. Virginia held her breath as the Indians began to pole the loaded raft away from the river bank.

"They'll sink them when they get to the middle," she whispered to Billy, who snickered in reply. "There must be another way to get across the river, " Virginia thought in a panic, and she and Billy rode off to find Pa.

"The Caws aren't like Grandma Keyes' Indians," Pa said, when Virginia finally found him preparing the Reed wagons for the crossing. "They make their living from folks who pay them to get safely across the river on their rafts. They won't sink us, Virginia, because if they did, they wouldn't get paid." But Virginia wasn't so sure, and when it was the Reeds' turn to be ferried across the river, she rode inside the wagon with her back to the wall so that no Caw could sneak up behind her.

It took almost a whole day to ferry the wagons across the river. Many of the emigrants, including the Reeds, camped on the banks of the Caw River that evening. By then, Virginia was getting used to the presence of the competent Indians, who had ferried every wagon across the river that day without sinking one. Pa was right--these Caws were not like Grandma Keyes' Indians.

But the next morning Virginia was startled when one of the Caw men snuck up behind them as she and Patty and Eliza were brushing their teeth on the riverbank. Virginia saw the Indian's face reflected in the river, and she spun around, spitting the water from her mouth practically on the Indian's feet. Patty saw him next and cried out a tiny "Oh," but Eliza continued to brush her teeth after giving the Indian a small nod of greeting. To Virginia, the Caw looked scary with his long braids and bronze skin. He was young, perhaps not much older than herself, and he didn't have a tomahawk, Virginia saw right away. He pointed at the toothbrush Virginia held in her hand, and said in perfect English, "Can I look?"

Virginia handed him the toothbrush and he examined it closely, turning it over and running his fingers over the wet bristles. Several other Caws ambled down to the river's edge to join them, and now they all had to examine Virginia's toothbrush, as well as Patty's and Eliza's.

"It's use is to clean the teeth?" asked one of the Caws.

"Actually, it's a machine newly invented just for those of us heading west. You see, we find the meat in this country rather tough, and the brush helps to sharpen the teeth," Eliza said.

The Indians began to speak amongst each other then in their own language, but Virginia could tell they were still discussing the toothbrushes. And then one of them did an incredible thing, something that no Indian in Virginia's imagination or dreams had ever done--he smiled. In Virginia's mind, all Indians were either angry or, at best, grim. Virginia smiled back at the Indian who held her toothbrush.

"It's a toothbrush," said Virginia. "You can keep it."

"We have no trouble eating our meat. You keep it. You'll have much need for it before you reach California." And he handed Virginia her toothbrush. Now Virginia was no longer afraid of Indians, so there was nothing else to dread about the rest of the journey.

As they made their way across Kansas, Virginia spent most of her time riding Billy, but she did not ride alone for she and Patty had found friends in two boys who were traveling with them. Fourteen-year-old John Breen and his brother, thirteen-year-old Edward, were two of the many children whose families had joined the wagon caravan since Independence. Barney, Tracker, Trailer and Tyler, as well as the Breen hound, Towser, often romped beside them as they rode across the flat Kansas landscape.

The Breens were Irish--foreigners, Ma had told Virginia. Virginia had asked John what it felt like to be a foreigner.

"We're not foreigners, Virginia. My Pa's been a citizen for two years and he can read and write, too," said John. Virginia didn't think of "foreigner" as being a bad thing, but apparently John did. And so, thought Virginia, did Ma who also called the Breens "those Catholics." Being Catholic must not be such a bad thing because when Virginia asked John about his religion, he did not deny being Catholic the way he denied being a foreigner.

Like the Reeds, the Breen family had three wagons. The Breens had sold their farm in Iowa to go west to find a better, easier life. Not so very different from the Reeds, after all, Virginia thought even if they were Catholic.

John's parents Patrick and Peggy had seven children. John, the oldest, was big for his age, but smart and thoughtful. Virginia also thought him very handsome. In fact, Virginia thought the addition of the Breen family to the caravan was the best thing that had happened to her, since the day that Pa gave her Billy. Edward Breen, an animal lover like Patty, seemed devoted to Virginia's younger sister, despite the difference in their ages. The Reed girls and the Breen boys spent the balmy days of late May riding together over the plains on their ponies, the dogs racing along behind. One day as they galloped along to scout out the trail ahead, Pa overtook them on Glaucus.

"You must return to the wagon at once," he said. "Grandma Keyes has died."

CHAPTER 4
The War Party

The entire caravan had delayed a full day while the men cut down a cottonwood tree and built a coffin for Grandma Keyes. They buried her under a large oak, and a minister who was traveling with them said a prayer over the grave. Another emigrant, a stonecutter from Springfield, found a large gray stone on which he carved, "Sarah Keyes; born in Virginia." Virginia and Patty planted wild flowers on the grave.

When the service was over, Virginia held Patty as she sobbed. Both girls were sitting on Grandma Keyes' feather bed, empty now. Cash jumped up on the bed and snuggled next to Patty and nosed her hand, whimpering. Patty stroked his silky head, and when she stopped caressing him he looked up at her and whined, demanding her attention.

Some of the emigrants complained at the day's delay, claiming that the caravan was already moving too slowly to make it over the mountains before winter. So, the Reed family screwed up their courage and headed west once again. In June they crossed the flat dusty territory called Nebraska, and Virginia's enthusiasm for the trip returned as she began to see land and wildlife that were new to her. One day she saw a herd of strange deer-like animals grazing on the plains as they approached. When the animals sensed their nearness, the animals ran so fast they seemed to fly or skim the ground with their graceful, buoyant strides. Pa said they were antelope.

Virginia's brothers, Jim and Tommy, were amused by the hundreds of comical little prairie dogs. The squirrel-sized animals stood straight as soldiers on mounds of dirt that they had dug out for their underground homes. They barked warnings to each other and disappeared into their homes whenever one of the boys or dogs came too near. Try as they would, the boys were never able to capture one of these animals. Not even the experienced hunting dog Barney had been able to capture one of these amusing animals.

But far more interesting to Virginia were the herds of buffalo that roamed through this country--great herds of them grazing the hot, treeless plains.

"The Indians use the hides of those buffalo for their beds," Eliza told Virginia. "They stuff their mattresses with the fur--just like we stuff our mattresses with feathers."

"Indians don't sleep on mattresses, Eliza," said Virginia, who remembered that Grandma Keyes' Aunt Mary refused to sleep on a bed after she had been released from captivity.

"Sure they do. Stuff 'em with grass and buffalo fur--that's what they call "prairie feathers" in this country," said Eliza. Virginia laughed.

In the evenings, the younger children made a game of collecting the dried buffalo scat, called "chips" which, in the absence of wood, they used for fuel. But Virginia was far more interested in hunting the buffalo than in gathering the chips. Buffalo meat was now their chief source of protein, and Virginia thought it tasty and tender.

"Please, Pa, let me go with you when you hunt," Virginia pleaded. But Ma had said absolutely not, that it was far too dangerous a pursuit for a young girl. But one evening when Pa and Virginia were out riding, they came across a small herd of buffalo. Pa and Glaucus started after them, and because Pa hadn't said she had to stay behind, Virginia and Billy took off after them. Virginia thrilled as she chased the huge animals across the plains, urging Billy on. If only she had a gun, then she could provide the meat for dinner. Wouldn't Ma be proud of her!

Suddenly, the herd thundering forward in front of her swerved, and Virginia realized with horror that the animals were headed straight for the camp. Pa quickly changed direction and rode for the herd's flank, trying to head them in another direction. "Follow Glaucus," Virginia urged as Billy surged forward.

Soon, she could see the camp, with the wagons at rest and the people starting the campfires for cooking the evening meal. As the herd neared the wagons, someone in the camp raised an alarm and Virginia saw mothers gathering children together and people jumping into the wagons, knocking things down in their haste to find safety from the stampede that descended on them in a cloud of dust. Virginia watched, horrified, and then, miraculously, the herd veered off to the right and galloped past the wagons. The buffalo herd was safely over the horizon as Virginia and Pa rode into camp.

Virginia couldn't remember ever seeing her delicate mother so angry, but now Ma was furious. "That was some of your work, Virginia. You'll not be riding Billy again until I say so."

"But Margaret, the girl didn't set out to chase that herd. We just came upon them," Pa said, and Virginia loved him for trying to defend her. But Ma was as angry with Pa as with Virginia.

"You'll be spoiling that girl till she's no good," said Ma in a sharp voice Virginia had never before heard her use with Pa. Virginia guessed that would be the end of her buffalo hunting.

By the end of June, the wagons reached Wyoming. They had hoped to reach the Rockies by the fourth of July, but Uncle Jake said they were a week behind, even though it seemed to Virginia that they were making good progress. They now followed the slow moving Platte River, crossing and recrossing it as they followed the route west. One day as they rested and restocked supplies at Fort Laramie, Pa had a visit from his old friend James Clyman, who had stopped at the fort on his return from California. Patty and Virginia sat quietly inside the wagon listening to their conversation.

"Reed, I'm warning you. Stay on the regular trail and never leave it. The cutoff you're thinking about is impossible this late in the year," said Clyman.

"Hastings says the cutoff will save us four hundred miles--we'll be able to make up for lost time and cross the Sierra before snowfall closes the pass," said Pa.

"I'm telling you Reed, Hastings is a fool. I was with Hastings when we scouted out that route, and no wagon train can get through it," said Clyman.

But Pa was stubborn once he'd made up his mind about something. "There is a nearer route, and it is of no use to take so much of a roundabout course," he said.

"You take the cutoff and you'll have to cross a desert before you reach those mountains. Can't carry enough water to get all these wagons and animals over that desert at one time. Once you get across it, you still have the Sierra Nevada to cross. Snow comes early and often up there. You get stuck in those mountains and you'll never get out alive," said Clyman.

Virginia felt her arms prickle with a chill even though it was warm inside the wagon. She exchanged a glance with Patty, whose eyes were big with fear. At their feet Cash twitched and whimpered as he chased prairie dogs in his dreams.

In mid July, Ma allowed Virginia to resume riding Billy, and Virginia was grateful to be out in the open air once again. Often, Patty sat behind Virginia as Billy carried them along the trail or across the prairie. Frequently, John and Edward Breen accompanied them, and for Virginia, those were the best of times. The wagons moved so slowly that there was time for rides off the trail, although Ma said they should be cautious not to stray too far away because the Sioux were on the warpath against their old enemies, the Blackfoot and the Crow. At Fort Laramie, they had watched as hundreds of Sioux performed a war dance, chanting to the beating of drums, brandishing their tomahawks in imitation of what they would do to their enemies. The next day, the Sioux had woven ribbons and feathers into the manes and tails of their horses, and then they formed a line almost three miles long. Pa told Virginia that the Sioux warriors would soon take their women and children to a safe place for the duration of the war.

"They shouldn't bother us too much if they're preoccupied with their own war," said Ma. "Still, don't go too far off the trail, and leave the dogs with the wagons. Some Indians will run off with anything they can steal," warned Ma. But Virginia had already met the enemy back at the Caw River and she was not afraid of Indians any longer.

One day, Virginia and Patty were riding with the Breen boys, staying close to the trail but just out of sight of the wagons. They had brought food and planned to share a midday meal before rejoining the wagons. When they found a good picnic spot, they spread a blanket and ate the dried buffalo meat and bread that Eliza had baked the evening before. After watering the horses and taking a cool drink themselves, they rested on the blanket in the hazy sunshine. In the distance, they could see the dust stirred up by the approaching wagon train. Virginia lay on her back and dozed and when she opened her eyes she was startled to see John leaning over her, gazing into her eyes. Was he going to kiss her right here in front of Patty and Edward who stood a short distance away tending to the horses? She closed her eyes and held her breath. Then she felt John's breath in her ear.

"We're being watched," he whispered.

Watched by Patty and Edward, he means, but no. She sat up and as her head whipped around, she came face to face with a Sioux in full war paint standing not more than six feet from the blanket. And just as suddenly, he was gone. At first, Virginia thought that she had dreamed the whole thing, but John assured her that the Sioux had been real even though Patty and Edward had not seen him. Quickly, they packed up their belongings and rode back to the wagons.

Some of the emigrants became alarmed at the closeness of the Sioux. Pa and the other men cleaned their guns in readiness, "just in case they should want to disturb us," he said. That night as they were eating their supper, a small band of Sioux rode quietly into the camp, so peacefully that only a few of the men jumped to fetch their guns. The Sioux were painted on their faces and chests. They wore leggings and huge feather headdresses, and Virginia wondered how these hats stayed on their heads when they galloped across the plains on their horses. But the Sioux did not seem interested in starting a war with them. The warriors looked around and then left. The next day, Virginia packed her spyglass and, mounting Billy, headed to the front of the wagon train where she could search the horizon for any more sign of the Sioux.

At noon, Pa rode up to fetch her. A Sioux war party had been following behind the wagons, he said, and Ma thought it best if Virginia rode inside the pioneer palace car, just to be safe. Disappointed, Virginia joined Ma, Patty, her brothers, Eliza and Cash in the wagon. That evening, the Sioux paid them another visit. This time there were twice as many warriors, and some of them swarmed around the pioneer palace car, looking and touching, as if it was a great curiosity. Virginia watched from inside the palace car with her family and Eliza. Pa stayed outside to keep an eye on the animals, which he said Indians were known to steal.

Ma sat calmly mending a sock. Eliza sat with Tommy on her lap. Virginia, Patty and Jim peered out the opening at the end of the wagon so they could get a good look at the Sioux. Cash raced around their feet, barking.

"We could give them our toothbrushes--make them go away," said Eliza, who appeared amused by all the commotion.

"We've plenty to trade with the Indians if it comes to that," said Ma. "I think they are just curious." She put her sewing aside and lifted Cash to her lap to quiet him.

Some of the Sioux had dismounted and were looking at themselves in the mirror that Eliza hung on the outside of the wagon every evening so she could primp. Virginia wanted to get a better look, so she leaned out of the opening a little way and pulled her spyglass out of its case. With a snap, she extended the glass and focused it on the nearest Sioux, who happened to be admiring himself in Eliza's mirror. Startled at the snap and no doubt thinking the spyglass was some kind of weapon, the warrior jumped on his horse and rode away, taking his friends with him.

Cash began barking again as the horses galloped away.

"There, Ma, you see. I fought off a whole Sioux war party with nothing but a spyglass!" said Virginia.

But Virginia's delight was dampened when Pa returned to the wagon.

"Virginia, it's Billy the Sioux want. They've never seen a pony like him--offered me buffalo robes and several of their own horses just to have him," said Pa.

"They can't have Billy! You won't let them take him, Pa."

"Of course not. I'll have one of the men ride Billy until we get through Sioux country. You'll have to ride in the wagon until then," said Pa. Although she was disappointed at having to ride in the stuffy wagon, Virginia knew Billy would be safest with an armed man riding him during the day. At night, Virginia would make sure Billy was tied up where she could see and hear him, and she would make sure she always carried her spyglass.

PART II
Troubles on the Trail

...never take no cutoffs and hury along as fast as you can.

Virginia Reed
(in a letter to her cousin written in the spring of 1847).

CHAPTER 5
The Hastings Cutoff

By July 20 the wagons had crossed the Rockies. It was an easy crossing. Why, if that's all there was to crossing a mountain range, what could be so bad about the Sierra Nevada, thought Virginia. They were almost halfway to California, even if they were moving so slowly that some of the travelers complained. Now they had a decision to make, and they consulted their elected leader, James Reed.

"If we leave the main trail now and take the cutoff Hastings recommends, we'll save a month and get over the Sierra Nevada by September," Pa said at a meeting in late July.

"Clyman says wagons can't get over the cutoff, Reed. We'll lose even more time if we have to backtrack to the main trail," said Hiram Miller, George Donner's teamster. Some of the men and women nodded in agreement.

A woman's voice lifted above the men's voices. "Why should we take a chance on leaving the old road, just on the word of an adventurer?" Virginia was surprised to see that the speaker was Tamsen Donner, Uncle George's wife. Uncle George, like Pa, favored taking the Hastings route, but his wife apparently did not.

"I say we stick to the main trail," said another.

Pa stood up on a rock and held up the Hastings guide book. "I have it as a personal promise from Hastings himself that the cutoff will get us to California faster." Pa reached into his shirt pocket and pulled out a letter and he held it up. "In this letter written just last month and delivered to me on the trail, Hastings says he will backtrack from Fort Bridger and escort us through the shortcut himself if we fail to find the way." After that, it seemed that more people seemed to favor Pa's route.

"Let's take a vote," suggested Mr. Breen. All men 15 and older could vote. Somehow, it didn't seem right that young boys practically her own age could vote on a matter that affected them all while grown women such as her own mother and Tamsen Donner were not allowed to cast a ballot. When the ayes and nays were counted, most sided with Pa--they would take the cutoff recommended by Lansford Hastings. But in another vote, they elected Uncle George Donner instead of Pa to lead them.

"They're angry that it has taken us so long to get here--that's why they elected a new leader," Pa explained. Pa was disappointed at not being the leader, but he had his way about something more important--the wagon train would follow the Hastings cutoff. Hiram Miller, in spite of the vote, refused to take the cutoff and left the Donners' employ that very night.

On the last day of July, the Reeds, Donners and Breens set out on the new route. The families who went with them included young Mr. and Mrs. Eddy from Illinois and their two young children. The Murphy clan from Tennessee also went with them. Lavina Murphy was a widow with five half-grown unmarried children. Her two married daughters and their husbands and children accompanied her. Ma in particular took a disliking to Mrs. Murphy and said she was "rough." Virginia saw that Mrs. Murphy was uneducated but not afraid to speak her mind no matter what anyone thought. Virginia thought her very brave to set out on such a journey without a husband.

A German family, Mr. and Mrs. Keseberg and their two young children and a companion, old Mr. Hardkoop, also went with them on the new route. Mr. Keseberg was a large man with a fiery temper, and few of the other travelers liked him, including Virginia. For one thing, he frequently beat his young wife. One time, Virginia had seen Mr. Keseberg slap his wife and then shove her into the river because she had burned the stew. Mr. Keseberg had pushed his wife so hard that she had stumbled and then fallen on her hands and knees into the muddy shallows. Virginia told Pa what she had seen, and Pa had words with Mr. Keseberg later that same day. Mr. Keseberg had told Pa to mind his own business.

Another time, while they were still following the Platte River, the wagon train had passed near a Sioux burial ground. The Indians had built tall scaffolds, and then wrapped their dead in buffalo robes and placed them upon these platforms. Mr. Keseberg had climbed up one of these scaffolds to steal a particularly fine buffalo robe. After a hasty meeting with the other men, Pa had confronted Keseberg and demanded that he return the robe to the scaffold and leave the grave as he found it.

"We cannot afford to offend the Sioux--they are already on the warpath, and they could just as easily turn their anger on us," Pa had said. Keseberg had told Pa to mind his own business that time, too, but the others finally persuaded Mr. Keseberg that to return the robe was in the best interest of everyone.

The group also included several single men, including Virginia's favorite, a middle-aged bachelor named Charles Stanton. Mr. Stanton was educated in geology and botany, and he enjoyed pointing out the sights to Virginia as she rode beside him on the trail. Mr. Stanton rode his mule, Betsy, because he said mules were hardier than horses, though not as fast, he admitted.

As the emigrants followed the Hastings route, Virginia, riding Billy, found much to marvel at. There were vast seas of sage and little streams that ran as red as blood. Mr. Stanton explained that the red color was from the minerals that dissolved in the water that drained down the mountains. He pointed out little bubbling springs with queer tasting water, and towering cliffs the height of which awed Virginia. Never in her days in Illinois had she seen such marvels. But the travel was becoming more difficult. The wagons sometimes had to be unhitched and lifted with ropes straight up the cliffs. They barely made two miles a day. And then abruptly, the trail ended. It was Virginia who found the letter from Hastings stuck in the bushes beside the road.

"Hastings writes that the Weber Canyon is very bad going. He asks us to send a messenger ahead where he waits for us. He promises to return with the messenger and show us a new route across the Wasatch Mountains," said Pa when the emigrants had been gathered together.

The men grumbled, talking amongst each other. "We should go back to the main trail before it's too late," said one. "We should return to Fort Bridger and wait out the winter there," suggested another. "Send Reed to find Hastings--this is all his doing," suggested another. Once again, they called a meeting to decide the best thing to do.

In the end, the emigrants decided to send Pa ahead to find Hastings and bring him back to guide them. That afternoon, Pa clattered away down the canyon on Glaucus. The others settled down to rest and to wait. But Pa did not return the next day, as promised, or the next, or the next.

"What if something has happened to Pa?" Virginia asked her mother on the fourth day after he left.

"Your father will return. He would never leave us here, Virginia," said Ma.

"But how do you know that, Ma'" Virginia asked.

"I just know," she replied.

Then on the fifth day, Pa returned. His face and arms were scratched and bruised and he looked tired and discouraged. Pa was not riding Glaucus, and he was alone. The travelers swarmed around Pa, eager for news. "Where is Hastings?" everyone asked.

"Hastings could not come. But I've spoken with him and he has shown me the way to go. We cannot get the wagons through Weber Canyon. We must take another way over the Wasatch," said Pa. Some of the travelers agreed with Pa that they should push ahead on the shortcut Hastings suggested, but others, including many of the women, favored returning to Fort Bridger. That night the men took a vote and decided to take the route that Hastings had shown Pa. When that had been decided, Virginia sought out her weary father.

"Where is Glaucus?" Virginia asked him.

"He gave out, Virginia. This country is too rough on a horse like Glaucus. He was meant for racing, not climbing," said Pa. Virginia hoped this country wouldn't prove to be too rough for a pony like Billy.

The next morning they set out. The route was rocky and overgrown, and much of the time the road had to be cleared with axes and shovels as they went. It was slow progress for three days, and many of the men began to blame Pa for their trouble. Then, when it seemed that they had no more energy left to chop through the cottonwood and aspen that blocked their way, they were surprised by three wagons that overtook them on the trail. The newcomers were the Graves family, a husband and wife with their nine children, ranging in ages from one to 22, and a son-in-law. With them also was their teamster, a young man named John Snyder.

"Heard back at Fort Bridger that the Donner party was taking a shortcut. Decided to leave the main trail and join you," said Mr. Graves. There, you see, Virginia thought smugly. Pa's decision wasn't so bad--other travelers had faith in Hastings' guide book too. Another good thing about the Graves joining them was that now there were four more adult men who could help clear the road ahead of them. They welcomed the Graves family and pushed on.

Virginia had stopped riding Billy, seeing that the way was too steep and rough for him by himself, let alone with a rider. Every morning as she fed and watered her precious pet, she stroked his face and talked to him, encouraging him to go on. Where once she had asked Billy to take care of her, now she promised to take care of him.

"Maybe we'll reach the end of the Wasatch today, Billy. Hold on, boy, and I'll give you a special treat when we make camp tonight. We'll be riding together in California before you know it," she whispered in the little horses's ear. He bowed his head as if to say he would do his best. But then one day, sore and lame, his sides heaving with exhaustion, Billy just stopped walking,. He lay down by the side of the road and would not get up. Pa came to Virginia and held her close.

"Go ride in the wagon, daughter," Pa said, and Virginia did not argue. She knelt beside the pony and wrapped her arms around Billy's neck, burying her face in his neck to breathe in the scent of him one more time and cried. Then she rose and went to the wagon as Pa had told her to do. Virginia sat in the back of the wagon and watched as Billy became smaller and smaller as they drove on. Finally she could see him no more.

CHAPTER 6
Desert Crossing

When the worn out travelers finally reached the bottom of the canyon, they were discouraged to see that next they would have to climb the sheer steep wall of a rocky cliff. Using two teams of oxen, they pulled each wagon straight up the canyon wall. Virginia held her breath as the pioneer palace car was hoisted. If just one of the oxen slipped, the wagon and both teams of oxen would fall 300 feet to the creek below. Somehow, all the wagons made it safely up the cliff without a mishap. It had taken them 21 days to move 36 miles, but they had finally crossed the Wasatch and reached the Salt Lake Valley. They stopped to rest and make repairs.

The next day they followed the trail again, an easy stretch of route through strange country, the likes of which Virginia had never seen. Sometimes, the trail led across the hills in order to avoid the marshes below. One evening, as they made camp in a valley dotted with springs full of cold water, Virginia sought out her friend, John Breen. Together they went to the springs to get fresh water for the horses.

"These seem more like wells than springs," said John as he filled his pail from the largest spring. The water holes varied from six inches to nine feet across. When John drew out his pail of water, the hole immediately filled up again, yet no water spilled over the edge as it would from a natural spring.

"This is strange country, John. Even water doesn't act like it should in this land," said Virginia.

Later that evening, the children played a game in which they tried to guess the depth of each water hole. Using a rope for measure, Virginia lowered it nearly seventy feet into one of the water holes, but the rope never found the bottom.

The next day they followed the trail to the edge of the desert where they stopped to prepare for the "dry crossing," for they would be days without water except for what they could carry. When the Reed and the Donner families camped side by side that night, it was Tamsen Donner who spotted the signboard with the tattered fragments of paper nailed to it.

"Strange place for a board in the middle of this wild country," said Tamsen, picking up the board that lay beside the road. Scraps of paper were stuck to the surface, and Virginia could see that the paper had writing on it.

"It's some kind of message," said Uncle George. Virginia and Patty began to pick up other pieces of paper that lay scattered on the ground--they all had writing on them.

"Let's see if we can piece this together," said Tamsen. She sat down with the board on her lap and using it as a table, began to arrange the scraps of paper. The others stood over her shoulder as she worked. Aunt Tamsen had been a schoolteacher and she was good with words, Virginia knew. In California, Tamsen planned to start a new school.

Virginia looked over Tamsen's shoulder now and began to read aloud the message taking shape on the board. "Two days and two nights. Hard driving. Cross desert. Reach water. Lansford Hastings."

"If Hastings says it will only take two days for the dry crossing, we should get started right away," said Pa.

"Two days and two nights, James. Do we push on in the dark? Is that what he means?" Ma asked.

"Such a brief message. Hastings might have told us more of what to expect in the desert," said Tamsen. Virginia wondered if more of the message might have been lost, or maybe destroyed by Indians or animals. She looked around on the ground for more paper fragments but found nothing.

That night, Uncle George Donner called a meeting and the travelers discussed how to best prepare for the desert crossing.

"Two days and nights of travel--that's 50 miles or more before we reach the next grass and water, " said Uncle George. Virginia sat with Tamsen Donner and Ma, listening as the men discussed quantities of water and food that would have to be carried with them to sustain people and animals while they journeyed across the desert. Both food and water would have to be carefully rationed as they went along.

"There's good grass and water in this valley. Maybe we should winter here and not try to cross the desert now," said Tamsen Donner. Nobody seemed to hear her.

The next day, the men began hauling water and loading it into the wagons. Eliza and Ma cooked enough food to last two days because there would be no time to cook nor fuel with which to start a fire once they were in the desert.

Virginia, Patty, and Jim cut grass in the meadows and then bundled it for the oxen to eat. On September 1 they began the "dry crossing." They drove most of the first day across a flat expanse of land. The sage brush grew sparser as the country got drier, and by late afternoon, they were at the foot of the hills they had seen in the distance. Up close, the trail appeared to rise steeply. Hastings had not told them that there would be mountains in the middle of the desert. Everyone got out of the wagons to lighten the load. Eliza and Virginia took turns carrying little Tommy. The oxen strained, pulling the wagons now heavy with the barrels of stored water, up and up before they finally topped the pass.

At the top of the mountain, Virginia looked down on the flat, glittering plain of salt that they still had to cross. Far as her eye could see, the sparkling white desert stretched out before them. They began the descent and reached the plains by nightfall when Virginia helped Pa to dole out the ration of water to the oxen. As darkness fell, a bone chilling cold settled over the desert, but the emigrants pushed on, not daring to rest. Two days AND two nights, Lansford Hastings had written.

On the second day, they faced an even more tortuous ridge than they had crossed the day before. The oxen toiled over the steep, rocky ground. Once over the ridge, the oxen sank almost knee deep in light, fine sand as they strained to pull the heavy wagons over the dunes. Ahead, they could see the mountains that would mean the end of the "dry crossing," but it didn't seem as though they were getting any closer to the mountains.

As Virginia plodded along on foot, the dust stinging her eyes and nostrils, she suddenly saw 20 girls in plains uniforms marching in single file in front of her. She stopped and stared. The parade of girls stopped. Virginia began to move towards them. The girls began to move away. What kind of game was this, she wondered. Then she realized that a mirage was tricking her.

The most heavily loaded wagons belonged to the Reeds and the Donners, and by afternoon of the second day they began to fall behind the others as the oxen weakened or gave out altogether. But they kept moving, through the second day and the second night. On the third day, the mountains still appeared a great distance away. They had prepared for only two days and two nights of hard travel, and now the water was almost gone. Ma and Eliza doled out the water to the children in small amounts. Patty cried when Ma said the dogs should not be watered at all that day.

That night as they pushed onward across the desert, the younger children began to cry out for water. Tamsen Donner gave the Donner and Reed children small lumps of sugar moistened with peppermint.

"The sugar will trick your thirst into going away," she promised. Although Virginia sucked on the sugar lumps, she still had a raging thirst, but the younger children quieted some. Finally, the sugar lumps ran out, and Aunt Tamsen gave them flattened bullets to chew on "to keep your mouths from feeling so dry."

At the end of the third day, the oxen could go no further. The water was just about gone, and all the cooked food except for a little bread had been eaten. Ma was suffering from one of her sick headaches but she kept going and did not complain. Hungry and thirsty, the children cried and the dogs whined. More of the oxen died, and the Reed wagons fell behind the others as their remaining oxen became too exhausted to push on. Finally, Pa ordered Milt to unyoke the tired oxen and drive them forward without the wagons until they found water.

"I will ride ahead on my horse and bring back water for you all," Pa promised the family. "You stay with the wagons and take care of your mother and the young ones," he said to Virginia before he set out on horseback across the great salt plain, once again leaving his family behind. Milt unyoked the poor, exhausted oxen and drove them along the trail behind Pa.

Virginia watched them disappear off the trail. How far could it be, wondered Virginia. They had already traveled three days and three nights, and Hastings had said two days and two nights. Surely Pa would find water and be back by nightfall. And after the oxen were watered, they would return refreshed enough to carry them out of the desert.

Darkness descended on the wagon, and Virginia tried to sleep curled up beside Patty for warmth. Outside, a cold wind blew sand against the canvas sides of the wagon. Virginia finally fell into a deep, dreamless sleep. At dawn, she was awakened by Cash, barking and barking at the wagon entrance. Underneath the wagon, Barney and her pups began to bark and howl in a language that all the Reeds understood. The dogs were greeting Pa! Virginia leaped out of the wagon to greet her father. He had found water!

"But where is Milt?" asked Ma. "And what about the oxen--did they make it to the water?"

"Milt and I became separated before we reached the water, Margaret," said Pa. "We have to have faith that Milt will soon return with the oxen."

Until Milt returned, they were stranded in the desert.

CHAPTER 7
Death on the River

All day, the Reed family and Eliza watched the desert trail for Milt's return. The sun beat down, and the only respite was to take advantage of the shade inside the wagon, although the air was dusty and stale. The dogs took cover under the wagon. Now the water Pa had brought back was beginning to run out. Tommy and Jim begged for a drink, but Virginia and Patty, understanding better what plight they were all in, made the best of their rations without complaint.

"We can't stay here through the night. As soon as it's dark, we'll set out on foot. Jacob Donner's wagon is just a few miles ahead of us on the trail. We'll go to them," said Pa as the sun began to sink over the desert horizon.

Ma, who was still not feeling well, rose from her bed and began to pack up what provisions were left, as well as the money quilt and knitted shawls to keep them warm. As soon as it was dark, the Reeds and Eliza set out on foot. Pa carried Tommy, and the five dogs trotted along behind them. Soon, a cold wind began blowing, and Pa thought it best to stop and rest for a while. He spread the money quilt on the ground and he and Ma and Eliza sat on it with their backs against the wind, sheltering the children. Pa covered them all over with the shawls and ordered the dogs to lie down next to them. The family spent a few hours of warmth and rest in this way before pushing on.

"Uncle Jacob's wagon should be just ahead. We'll see it any time now," said Pa, and sure enough, at daylight they came upon the Jacob Donner wagon with the family still sleeping inside. When Pa roused Uncle Jacob, he had more bad news for the Reeds.

"Milt was driving your oxen to the watering place, and well, they were crazy with thirst, you know. They smelled water and bolted. Just stampeded. Milt looked for them all day yesterday," said Uncle Jacob.

Pa put his head in his hands, and Ma stood by him with a hand on his back.

"I'll help you look for the oxen, Pa," Virginia. said, eager to do something, anything but sit inside a wagon one more day.

"Your Ma needs you to help with the boys, Virginia," said Pa.

"My oxen have been watered and rested, James. You go on and look for your team. I'll take your family out of the desert in my wagon," said Uncle Jacob.

After six days and six nights, all the emigrants made it out of the desert safely. Some of the people had walked out, carrying their children in their arms. Others, like the Reeds, had abandoned their belongings in the desert and had to be carried out in the wagons of the others. After they were rested, they would have to return to the desert to bring out the wagons they had left there. But first, Pa needed his oxen and after a week of searching, he and Milt still had not found the team.

"They've been gone too long. Stolen by Indians, probably. We'll never find them now," said Pa, discouraged.

"I'll loan you a team, Reed. It's all I can spare," said Mr. Graves. "It'll get one of your wagons out of the desert." Pa was grateful.

"But what of our furniture and our books and clothes?" asked Ma when Pa told her they would have to leave the pioneer palace car behind in the desert.

"We'll cache our belongings by burying them in the sand. One day, we'll come back for our things, I promise, Margaret," Pa said.

That morning, Pa and Virginia and Milt rode into the desert one last time. From the wagons, they took those things that were absolute necessities--food, cooking utensils, blankets, clothing--and loaded them into one of their smaller supply wagons. Then Milt drove the borrowed oxen hauling the heavily loaded wagon out of the desert.

Virginia took one last look around the abandoned pioneer palace car that had been her home since April, almost five months. She looked at Grandma Keyes' feather bed and the little stove that had warmed the inside of the wagon on the cool nights in Kansas. She saw Ma's sewing basket and Eliza's hairbrushes and the mirror that hung on the wall, and she thought it ironic that after all they had suffered that now they would have to leave all these comfort items in the desert.

Virginia decided she would take to the children whatever she could carry with her in her pockets. She gathered up Tommy's toy soldier, Jim's wooden knife and Patty's pocket skirt. Finally, she pocketed Cash's toy ball. Virginia and Pa packed their belongings into the bed of the pioneer palace car. Then they made a cache by digging a hole in the sand, and placed the bed of the wagon into the hole and buried it.

"Won't the Indians take our things, Pa?" Virginia asked. It didn't take much looking to see that the mound of sand covering the cache was built by people, not created by the wind. She didn't think it would fool the Indians at all.

"Maybe they will, maybe they won't. We still have money, Virginia, and with it we'll be able to buy what we need once we get to California," said Pa.

On September 26, the wagon train rejoined the main trail. The emigrants cursed Lansford Hastings for leading them astray. Shortcut indeed! They had lost valuable time by taking the route that Hastings recommended and now they were running short on food. The emigrants called a meeting and decided that someone would have to ride ahead to bring back food for them all or they would never make it to California. One of the men who volunteered was Virginia's trail companion, Mr. Stanton.

"I'll be back in a few days with enough food to get us all over the mountains to California," Stanton promised as he prepared his mule, Betsy, for the trip.

"But you'll be back much faster if you take your horse instead of riding Betsy," said Virginia.

"Mules are more surefooted on the rocks," he said to Virginia. Virginia guessed she knew as well as anyone how hard the mountain terrain was on a fine horse.

"But you can't always get a mule to do what you want. Betsy'll just take you where she wants to go," said Virginia.

"Betsy'll do my bidding, you'll see. We'll soon be back here with provisions enough for everyone, and I'll be riding Betsy and more mules'll be carrying the food," said Mr. Stanton.

"What's more, Virginia Reed, me and Betsy'll be back in time to carry you over the Sierra Nevada, and you can take my word for it." Then Mr. Stanton mounted Betsy and lumbered off on the trail ahead of them.

They now had only a few weeks left to make it over the Sierra Nevada before the heavy snows closed the mountain pass. The days grew shorter as September gave way to October. Game grew scarce, and one day when Mr. Eddy was out hunting antelope he was shot at by the Indians but returned unharmed. The same day several of the Reed's oxen were shot and killed by the Indians who fired down on them from the heights above. The very next night, several of the horses were stolen while the emigrants slept, and to the Reeds' sorrow, Barney and her pups disappeared. Sometimes, the travelers could see Indians watching them from the high places overlooking the trail. They seemed to be laughing at the travelers as they struggled along.

The weather was cooler, but tempers flared as the journey stretched out and they still had not reached California. Food was running low, but there was no word from Mr. Stanton and the others who had been sent ahead to bring back supplies. Where could they be?

On October 5 the wagon train approached a long, sandy hill that rose above the Humboldt River. The Donner wagons had crossed the hill successfully and were now out of sight of the others, far ahead on the trail. Next in line was the Graves wagon, driven by the hot tempered John Snyder, followed by the Reed wagon, driven by Milt. Halfway up the sandy incline, Snyder halted his team and Milt hollered "gee" as he tried to maneuver the Reeds' oxen around the Graves' wagon. Milt's lead ox grew excited on the narrow path and swerved into the Graves team.

"Whoa," Milt hollered to the team.

"What do you think you're doing," yelled Snyder, going nose to nose with Milt. Snyder's face was red with anger. Milt ignored him and tried to untangle the teams.

"Are you crazy, man? Passing me on this narrow trail. You're an idiot," Snyder raged, and he raised his whip as if to strike Milt, but then in anger he turned the whip upon his oxen team and began to beat the poor lead ox until it bellowed in pain. Virginia looked on in horror. All the wagons were stopped now, and people were running up the hill to see what was to be done. Pa rushed forward and grabbed Snyder's arm as Snyder was about to lay the whip on his oxen again.

"Take it easy, Snyder. No need to beat the animals--it was a mistake, that's all," said Pa. "Your idiot driver's mistake, Reed. And I'll beat my team if I want to. In fact, maybe I'll beat you too," said Snyder as he turned his rage on Pa. Virginia watched as Pa and Milt tried to reason with Snyder.

"I'll help you untangle the teams, Snyder. Just stop beating the animals," said Pa. Snyder cursed loudly and spat at Pa, who drew his hunting knife. Suddenly Snyder struck out at Pa with the butt of his whip, making a long gash across Pa's head. Blood spurted and ran down Pa's neck, soaking his shirt. Pa ducked to avoid another blow and as he did, he lunged at Snyder with his knife, plunging the weapon into Snyder's chest.

"No! Stop it, now," a woman shrieked, and Virginia was startled to see that the words had come from her own, quiet mother who had run up the trail and was now standing between Pa and Snyder. From behind, Milt pulled at Snyder, but Snyder shrugged him off and struck Ma with the whip and she fell on her hands and knees. Then Snyder hit Pa again, and Pa fell backwards onto the trail. Snyder was still on his feet, and Virginia saw him take a few steps up the hill toward his team before he staggered and fell.

Blood was running down Pa's face when Virginia and Ma reached him. Nearby, Mr. Graves and Mr. Eddy were tending to Snyder.

"I am dead," Virginia heard Snyder say. Pa covered his own bloody face with his hands, and when he removed them, Virginia was surprised to see that Pa was crying.

"I've killed a man," said Pa in a voice Virginia could hardly recognize and she reached out a hand to comfort him.

"He's not dead, Pa," said Virginia. "He's talking." She looked at the crowd gathered around Snyder. Pa tore himself away from Ma's embrace and flung his bloody knife away from him onto the trail, where it clattered down the steep hill and splashed into the river below.

"I'm sorry, so sorry. I didn't mean to kill you Snyder," said Pa. When Virginia scrambled up the hill to get a look at Snyder, she could see that the young man was indeed dead.

"I want justice, Reed," shouted Mr. Graves, who stepped in front of them on the trail. "My driver's dead. Now who will get my wagon to California?" Virginia could see that Mr. Graves was very angry. Pa just hung his head. Ma wept as Patty tried to comfort her. Eliza stood by the wagon holding tightly to each of Virginia's brothers' hands. Other voices joined with Mr. Graves, demanding justice for Snyder's death.

"Arrest Reed and hold him for trial in California," said Mrs. Murphy.

"There is no law in California!" protested another.

"Let's hang him right here!" hollered Keseberg. Several other men helped Keseberg prop up his wagon tongue with an ox yoke. One of them threw a noosed rope over the yoke and they began to move towards the Reeds. Virginia clung tightly to her father's arm. She wished that the Donners had not gone on so far ahead, for if they were here, Uncle George and Uncle Jacob would stand up for Pa.

"I deserve to die. I've killed a man," said Pa who just stood there beside Virginia as the men approached. He held up his head and confronted Keseberg and the others. "Come on then, hang me," said Pa. But not a man moved forward to take action.

"Hold on," shouted Mr. Eddy, his voice lifting above the din. "One death is bad enough. If we kill Reed, then there'll be two deaths, which is worse. Let's hold a meeting and talk this out and see what is a sensible punishment for Reed."

The others grudgingly agreed, as long as Pa was excluded from the meeting. While the meeting was being held, Virginia and her family returned to their wagon where Virginia washed the blood from her father's face and cleaned his wound. Ma wept softly as Eliza and Patty comforted the terrified Tommy and Jim. At evening, Mr. Eddy came to see Pa.

"Your life is to be spared, Reed, but you must leave the wagon train. That is the compromise we all agreed on," said Mr. Eddy.

"You're asking me to desert my family? What will become of them? They've done no wrong," said Pa.

Ma stood and put her arms around Pa. "You must go, James. To stay here would be certain death," she said.

"But how can I leave you? How will you get to California?" asked Pa.

"I will help to get your family safely to California, Reed. Milt has promised to stand by them and help out as needed. But you must leave tonight--for your own safety and for your family's. Tempers are hot. Keseberg is still for the hanging and he has others who agree with him," said Mr. Eddy.

"And what of my supporters? Who stood for me, Eddy?" asked Pa.

"Only myself and your driver, Milt," he replied. Everyone had liked the young Snyder even if he had been a hot head. Also, most of the travelers were still angry with Pa because of their trouble on the Hastings cutoff. They still blamed Pa.

"Do what you have to Reed, but do it fast. They're gathering to bury Snyder now, and that's bound to whip up more resentment against you," said Mr. Eddy.

Virginia moved around the wagon, gathering together the items her father would need to journey on alone.

"Reed, one more thing. You can't take your firearms with you when you go. That decision is part of your sentence," said Eddy.

No firearms! How would Pa get meat without his gun? And how would he defend himself against the Indians if they should decide to attack? Why, the banishment was no better than a death sentence, after all, thought Virginia.

And ahead of them all lay another desert.

CHAPTER 8
Something Awful

Ma and Virginia helped Pa bundle up a few clothes and a blanket to take with him. Ma urged him to take the packet of food she had packed.

"I won't be taking food out of my own children's mouths, Margaret. Don't worry. The Donners can't be more than a day's ride ahead on the trail. They will give me food and a gun," said Pa. Ma and Patty wept.

"I'll leave signs along the trail so you'll know that I'm OK," he promised. "You'll see, everything will be fine once we meet in California."

To his wife, Pa said, "Be strong, Margaret."

"Our children will not see tears in my eyes again unless they be tears of joy at your return," Ma promised.

And so Pa had kissed each member of his family and rode out of camp on a sorry looking pony, carrying nothing but his bundle of clothes and a blanket. It broke Virginia's heart to watch him disappear up the trail, but after he was out of sight, Virginia wasted no time in finding Milt.

"Milt, as soon as it gets dark, we'll follow Pa. We'll take him his rifle and ammunition and food. We'll take the mare for Pa. Then you can return with the pony and I'll ride on to California with Pa," said Virginia.

"Your Ma won't like it, Virginia," said Milt. Milt was kind, but slow thinking, and Virginia knew she could sway him to do what she wanted.

"We can't worry Ma right now. My plan is a sensible one, Milt. With both me and Pa gone, there will be enough food for Ma and the children and Eliza and you to last until Mr. Stanton returns," said Virginia.

Milt seemed to see the sense in Virginia's plan, and soon after dark Virginia and Milt rode quietly out of camp. The strong horse that carried both riders soon overtook Pa's tired little pony.

Pa was happy to see them. Virginia gave her father the rifle and ammunition and shared a little bread with him while she told him of her plan. Milt fed and watered the horse.

"Virginia, quite likely you've saved my life by bringing me my gun and ammunition, but you can't go on to California with me. You must go back to your mother," said Pa.

"Milt will take care of Ma and the children, if that's what you're worried about. I can ride on with you, we can get more food and then come back for Ma and the others," Virginia said.

"No, Virginia. You don't understand. Someone has to be in charge. Your mother is not well, and Milt, though he's a big, strong man, needs someone to tell him what to do. That person is you, Virginia. I need you to go back to the wagon," said Pa.

For the second time that day, Virginia said goodbye to her beloved father, and leading the pony, she and Milt walked back to the place where the wagons had stopped for the night.

The very next day Mr. Eddy stopped by the Reeds' wagon with more bad news.

"Your wagon is too heavy for the oxen, Mrs. Reed. The best plan is for you to transfer your belongings to a lighter wagon. Mr. Graves has offered one of his small wagons for that purpose," said Mr. Eddy. Virginia thought that the transfer was further punishment for Pa's killing of Snyder, but she didn't say as much to Ma. Instead, she helped Ma and Eliza transfer what few belongings they could take to the smaller wagon. Then Milt transferred the borrowed ox team to the borrowed wagon, and they drove on.

The boys rode the Reeds' one remaining pony, but everyone else had to walk. Even little Cash was forced to trot along beside his family, but when he grew too tired, Patty and Virginia took turns carrying him.

They still had not caught up with the Donners who must be far ahead of them on the trail. As they moved ahead, Virginia scanned the trail for signs of Pa. Virginia was encouraged when the wagon train came across a campfire still warm from the night before. Another time, they found a pile of feathers, and Virginia was convinced that Pa had dined on wild game the night before. And then, for several days, there were no signs. Virginia feared the worst.

Most of the travelers were on foot now to lighten the loads in the wagons and because so many of the horses and oxen had been lost or killed. Some of the emigrants had been forced to throw out their heavier possessions along the trail. Only 15 of the original 23 wagons remained.

One of the single men traveling with the Kesebergs, old Mr. Hardkoop, had become too weak to travel on foot and so was carried to the Keseberg wagon one morning when he just couldn't take another step. That evening when they stopped to camp, Mr. Hardkoop was missing. Virginia and John Breen went back along the trail to look for him and found him sitting under a sage bush.

"Keseberg told me to get out of his wagon," said the old man. Virginia and John helped Mr. Hardkoop mount the horse and they took him back to camp. The next day, Mr. Hardkoop came to Mr. Eddy and asked to ride in the Eddy wagon.

"Hardkoop, we'll be riding through sand for the next few miles--I don't think the oxen can take the extra weight through it. Ride with Keseberg for now and tell him that after we get through the sand, I'll take you the rest of the way in my wagon," said Mr. Eddy. They traveled on through the sand, and when they reached hard ground, Mr. Eddy went to fetch Mr. Hardkoop as he had promised.

"He rode with for me for a ways, and then I turned him out to walk," said Keseberg. "Don't worry, Eddy, he'll catch up with us sometime during the night."

"You're heartless, Keseberg," said Mr. Eddy, disgusted, and he set out to look for the old man, but soon returned alone. "Too dark to see and my horse is too weak. We'll look tomorrow if he doesn't show up during the night."

By the following morning Mr. Hardkoop had still not caught up with the rest.

"No use all of us wasting another day--we're a month behind already. I say the rest of us should go forward while a volunteer goes back to look for Hardkoop," suggested Mr. Breen.

"Will you go back to look for him then, Breen?" asked Mr. Eddy.

"My horse won't carry a man. She's about played out as it is. Someone else will have to go," said Mr. Breen.

But no one volunteered.

"'Tis murder to leave him behind," said Ma.

"The old man is probably dead, anyway. No use wasting valuable time backtracking," said Mr. Keseberg.

"Even if he's dead, the decent thing to do is to go back and bury his body," said Ma.

Mr. Keseberg turned towards the west and pointed at the mountains, already tipped in white. "There's snow in those mountains already--we've got to look out for ourselves now," he said. The others bowed their heads, either in assent or in shame. No one was willing to wait for another day while the Sierra Nevada was still to be crossed. Virginia thought it an awful thing.

PART III
Snow Upon Snow

The mothers were the real heroes...

--Patty Reed

CHAPTER 9
Trapped!

Finally, the last desert was crossed, and the weary travelers rested. Ahead of them lay the final barrier to California--the Sierra Nevada mountains, and before they crossed them they would need provisions.

"Where is Stanton?" was what everyone wondered. It had been a month since they had sent him ahead to California to return with the food they would need in order to cross the mountains.

"We'll never see Stanton again. He's a bachelor--what has he got to return for? He's already across the mountains," said Eliza to Virginia one day.

"He will bring us food. He promised. And he promised to carry me over the mountains on his mule," said Virginia.

Although they had lost all their oxen, the Reeds still had some of their beef cattle, what hadn't been killed or stolen by the Indians along the trail, but the animals were bony and weak. Eliza had scraped the bottom of their flour barrels to make the last loaf of bread, and they had eaten the last of the dried fruit. They desperately needed food but they could not afford to wait for Stanton in the valley when the Sierra Nevada had to be crossed. Already they could see snow at the peaks. They reached the Truckee River and began to toil up the rocky canyon.

Ma carefully provisioned the last of the jerked venison and coffee and Milt shot a wild goose, but that was all the food they had until Stanton returned with provisions. The other families weren't much better off. And then on the third day of their struggle up the canyon, Virginia spotted three riders and seven pack mules coming down the trail towards them. Virginia pulled her spyglass open and focused it on the riders.

"It's Mr. Stanton!"

As the riders came closer, she saw that two Indians rode with him, Mr. Stanton's guides through the mountains. The pack mules were heavily loaded.

"Food in camp!" shouted Stanton as he rode toward the wagons, and quickly the word spread down the wagon train that Mr. Stanton had returned. From the mule packs, he and the two Indians unloaded dried beef, flour, honey and corn meal. Tonight there would again be bread baking in camp! But to the Reeds, Mr. Stanton brought something even more precious than food--news about Pa.

"Your Pa made it to California--I saw him there," said Mr. Stanton to Virginia. "He had a rough go of it, but he wants you to know that he's organizing a relief party to meet you in the mountains with more provisions."

Pa was alive! And he was coming to get them. Virginia could hardly believe it. It had been weeks since they had seen a sign from Pa, and his family had feared that he was dead. Now it was late October and they still had to cross the mountains, but they would make it because Pa was coming to get them.

"There's early snows in the pass, but it's still passable. Won't close till November, most likely," said Stanton. "Best advice I can give is for you to stop and rest, let your oxen gather strength for the climb." For five days they rested in the Truckee Meadows at the base of the mountains. On the sixth day, Mr. Stanton took up Virginia behind him on Betsy as he had promised. Ma and Tommy rode on another mule. Patty and Jim and Eliza each rode behind one of the Spanish-speaking Indians. No longer would the Reeds have to walk, thanks to Mr. Stanton.

The snow began to fall as they moved through heavily forested country, and the air grew bitterly cold. At night the men cut tree boughs for the oxen and cattle to eat because the snow was too deep for the animals to graze. Their only guide was the summit of the mountain, but as the snow fell more heavily, the summit was covered by dark clouds. At one point on the trail near a lake, Mr. Stanton pointed out a cabin which he said was built by snowbound travelers the year before. But they would not get stuck in these mountains because Pa was coming to get them.

It kept snowing as they struggled on. The Donner wagons fell behind after Uncle George cut his hand with an ax.

"Go on ahead. We'll soon catch up," said Uncle George. The Reeds were sorry to be parted from their friends, but they kept going at Mr. Stanton's urging.

Soon, they lost the road as the snow piled in great drifts over the trail. The men set fire to a dead pine tree, and as the campfire warmed the travelers, they discussed what should be done.

"We must abandon the wagons and hurry over the pass. It's our only hope now. Once the snows start, they don't stop," said Mr. Stanton to the tired emigrants. Virginia looked up at the moon ringed with a pinkish light. Mr.

Stanton told her that the ring forecast even more snow. But everyone was tired and no one moved.

"I'm telling you, we must go now. Abandon the wagons, lift up the children and carry them over the pass --you'll all die if you get caught in these mountains in deep snow," said Mr. Stanton.

"We can't move now, Stanton," said Mr. Breen. "Let's rest for the night and get started in the morning." The others agreed with him, and that night Virginia's mother laid a buffalo robe on the ground to make a bed for them all. Virginia lay under the blankets and quilts as the snow continued to fall on them. Nearby, she saw one of the Indians wrapped in his own buffalo robe, standing under a tree, watching them. All night he stood under the tree. If Virginia had understood Spanish, she would have heard the Indian tell Mr. Stanton that they were all doomed.

The next morning, Virginia awoke to a foot of new snow that had fallen during the night. Big snowflakes still swirled down through the trees. It was impossible to move forward or turn back. They had waited too long and now they were trapped in the mountains. Discouraged, the emigrants decided their best chance of survival was to turn back and make camp by the lake they had passed the day before.

The Breens claimed the cabin that Mr. Stanton had pointed out to Virginia. Although it had a fireplace and chimney, there were no windows. The roof was made of ox hide and pine brush. The Kesebergs began to build a three-walled hut against one wall of the Breen cabin.

Milt and Mr. Stanton, aided by the two Indians, began to build a new cabin out of crooked logs. This cabin had a wall down the middle that would separate it into two rooms. They made the roof by laying down poles side by side and covering them with boughs, blankets and ox hides. Inside they built a rock fireplace. One room of this cabin would shelter the Reeds, Eliza, Milt, Stanton, the two Indians and Cash; on the other side of the wall would live the Graves family.

A third cabin was erected against a huge granite rock. Four families, including the Murphys and the Eddys, would take shelter here. The Donner families had never caught up with the others after Uncle George's accident, but they would also be trapped by the snows and have to make camp somewhere back on the trail. Milt promised to look for them when the Reed cabin was finished.

It took a week to build the shelters. Now it was November 11, and the snow had not let up at all. The next task was to slaughter the remaining cattle and oxen and freeze the meat in the snow for the coming winter.

"But we've no oxen or cattle left to slaughter, Mrs. Reed," said Milt to Ma.

"I shall provide meat for this family, Milt, make no mistake. My children will not starve," said Ma with a strength that surprised Virginia. Then Ma bundled into her warmest shawl and trudged through the snow to the Breen cabin. When she came back she said to Milt, "I have arranged with Mr. Breen to give him two cattle once we reach California for each one that he will give me here. We shall have beef for supper," said Ma. Milt slaughtered the cattle and put the meat into the snow to preserve it.

"With careful rationing, we should have enough meat for a month," said Ma, "and Milt may be able to shoot some game or catch fish in the lake." But meat and fish would not sustain them. The flour and fruit that Mr. Stanton brought back was nearly gone. Still, they wouldn't starve, Virginia thought. Surely Pa would come over the mountain to rescue them before the food ran out.

CHAPTER 10
Hunger and Hardship

By early December the snow lay eight feet deep and still it continued to fall. Mr. Breen slaughtered the last of his cattle and now the meat was gone. In the Reed cabin, Ma boiled the same bones over and over in the big black pot that was suspended over the fire. Sometimes the bones would actually soften enough to be chewed and swallowed. The tasteless, watery soup at least kept them from starving, but they were growing weaker.

Eliza especially seemed to be affected the most by the lack of decent food. Where she was once bright and lively, she now grew grim and short tempered. Eliza would often cry out in her sleep, waking them all in the crowded cabin. Her stories, once clever and fanciful, now grew desperate. One day Virginia had found Eliza digging a deep hole in the snow.

"They say the Indians make a kind of shortening out of earthworms. If I could just get to the earthworms, we could have bread," said Eliza, pawing frantically in the snow with her hands.

"Come Eliza, let's go back to the cabin and warm your hands. Even if you could dig though all that snow, the ground underneath is frozen, remember?" said Virginia, and she led a dazed Eliza back to the cabin.

The other families were not much better off than the Reeds. The men had not been able to find much game in the mountains, nor had they been able to pull fish from the icy waters of the nearby Truckee Lake. One day, however,

Mr. Eddy killed a huge grizzly bear and he generously shared the meat, but it didn't feed the starving emigrants for long. There were just too many of them.

There was also grim news about the Reeds' friends, the two Donner families. Milt had hiked back on the trail and found them camped in a swampy area about six miles away.

"They were able to build cabins for shelter?" asked Ma.

"George's hand isn't healing and Jacob's too sick to build a cabin. Had to take shelter in tents. They propped up some poles against a tree and covered them all over with quilts and canvas," said Milt.

In mid December, the emigrants who were camped by the lake met to discuss their situation. "Some of us must try to cross the pass on foot and bring back relief for the others," said Mr. Stanton. It seemed a good plan--the only plan that could save them. Seventeen people, including five women and two children, immediately volunteered to go.

"But how will you cross on foot, Stanton? The snow's too deep for walking," said Mrs. Breen.

"We'll snowshoe over the pass," said Mr. Graves. "Snowshoes will allow us to walk right on top of the snow. Done it myself plenty of times back in Vermont."

"But we don't have any snowshoes, Graves," said another.

Mr. Graves held up an oxbow. "We've no other use for these anymore. No ox left to yoke," he said. And Virginia could see that the oxbow was shaped something like the snowshoes that had hung on the barn wall back in Illinois.

During the next few days, Mr. Graves and Mr. Stanton worked to make the snowshoes that would carry the rescue party over the mountain snow. They wove strips of rawhide back and forth across the oxbow frames and finally they had 14 pairs of snowshoes that would hold a person's weight as he walked over the snow. The three without snowshoes would walk last, following the packed trail made by the snowshoers in front of them. In this way, all 17 volunteers who wished to go could make the trip over the mountains. They took six days' rations of food apiece. As Virginia watched the snowshoers trek off across the snow fields, led by Mr. Stanton and the two Indians, she felt a renewed hope. They were going to make it after all. If Pa failed to find them, surely Mr. Stanton and the others would be back to rescue them before Christmas.

They settled down to wait. In the Reed cabin, they ran out of food. "I will not let my family starve," said Ma, who pulled off a hide from their cabin roof. Virginia helped Ma to cut the dirty, unwashed hide into strips which they held over the fire to singe off the hair. Then the strips went into the stew pot to boil. There was no salt with which to season their soup, but when the mixture cooled, it thickened and filled their starving bellies. "It's like eating a pot of glue," said Virginia. Eliza refused to eat it, saying that it made her sick. If hunger and despair had once driven Eliza frantic, she was now past caring. They all grew weaker.

A few days before Christmas, Milt returned from a visit to the Donners with the news that Jacob Donner and three of the Donner teamsters had died. The Reeds wept at the loss of their friend.

"Did they starve?" asked Ma.

"They just lost hope and got sick," said Milt. "The rest are eating what we eat--buffalo hides and field mice, when they can catch them."

By Christmas week, all of the animals in the camp, including most of the dogs, had been eaten. Only the Reeds' Cash and the Breens' Towser were left. The children cried out in hunger. Ma made them drink water to keep a feeling of fullness in their stomachs. The days passed and still the rescue party did not return. And where was Pa?

"Your father will come for us," said Ma. "We must stay strong so he can lead us out of here." Never once did Virginia see her mother weep. She was keeping the promise she made to her husband on the day he had left. She would stay strong for the children.

By Christmas eve there was still no sign of rescue for the starving camp. Virginia thought back to earlier, happier Christmases when there were stockings to hang by the fireplace and lavish presents for everyone in the wealthy Reed family. No "Merry Christmas" greetings rang from the Truckee lake cabins on this Christmas morning. While Eliza sat staring at the fire, the Reed children and Milt and Ma shared their pot of glue for the breakfast.

"And we'll thank God first for providing us with it," said Ma as they sat down to eat. But after breakfast, Ma began to brighten up. First she heated a bucket of snow until it melted and then carried it out the door to a corner of the cabin. Carefully, she poured bucket after bucket of warm water into the snow, melting it down to a deep crater beside the cabin.

From the melted crater, Ma pulled out a cache of stored treats--dried apples, some beans, a square of beef tripe, and a small piece of salted bacon. Virginia's mouth watered as she watched. Her brothers laughed and sang out in anticipation. Cash whined for a treat and Patty scooped up the little dog into her embrace and he wriggled in delight. This would be a Christmas to remember after all!

"I determined when we first made this camp that my children would have a Christmas treat," said Ma as she put all of the feast ingredients into the stew pot, and soon the delicious aroma of the cooking food filled the cabin until Virginia thought she could no longer stand it. And then Ma pronounced the meal cooked and the Reeds, Milt and Eliza sat down to their Christmas dinner.

"Children, eat slowly, for this one day you can have all you wish," said Ma.

On the other side of the wall, the Graves family sat down to their meal of boiled bones and oxhide soup.

CHAPTER 11
Escape from Camp

During breaks in the snowfall, even though the cold was numbing, Virginia spent most of the daylight hours sitting outside with Patty. The sunlight sparkling on the snow would have been pretty under other circumstances, but the sisters were too weak and sick from lack of food to notice. They dragged themselves out of the cabin each sunny morning for one reason--to watch for Pa who was on his way to rescue them. Virginia and Patty lay on their backs in the snow, tasting only the river, the pines, and the wind, watching the high mountain pass for signs of movement that would mean that relief was on its way.

When the fierce snowstorms blew, the children stayed inside the crowded, smelly cabin with Ma and Milt and Eliza. They took their mood from the strength of the fire. When the fire blazed bright, warming them and bathing the inside of the cabin with a golden glow, Ma sewed and told stories from the Bible. Had they not been so hungry, they might have been cheerful in the ambience. But on days when blizzards howled around the cabin and they were so completely snowed in that they could not even leave the cabin to gather wood, Virginia and Patty and Milt chipped wood from the walls in order to keep the feeble fire going, and Ma spoke in fits and starts like the embers that snapped in the dying fire. In the iron kettle on the hearth simmered the glue pot stew, flavored only by the bits of twigs, bark, or leaves that they were able to forage during lulls in the storms.

One day as they sat in front of a feeble fire, Milt tapped his ax on one of the large rocks used as the fire iron. A small piece of the rock broke off and Milt picked it up to examine something that reflected the light as though the rock itself held a tiny fire inside it.

"Ma Reed, this is gold," he said, holding it out in the palm of his hand.

"I wish it were bread," said Ma.

Virginia and Patty helped Milt to hunt in the ashes for more shining particles, and soon they had gathered up about a teaspoonful, which Milt tied up in a small piece of buckskin and placed in his pocket.

"If we ever get out of here, I'm coming back for more," said Milt.

Virginia thought that if they ever got out of there, she'd never come back for anything.

Time dragged on and still no one came to rescue them. The roof hides were nearly gone, and there was nothing but a few blankets and tree boughs to keep the heavy snow from falling in on them. One day Ma sent the children outside with Milt for firewood and when they returned Ma told them that little Cash had died and must go into the soup kettle. Patty, who had loved Cash the most, cried and cried, but in the end, she ate the stew. Thanks to Cash, they would survive another week.

Often, Virginia was awakened by snow falling upon her face during the night. The cabin no longer provided them with shelter--they had literally eaten themselves out of their home. Where were the snowshoers who had promised to send help? Where was Pa?

"He's not coming. He thinks we're dead," said Virginia.

"He would never give up on us," said Ma. "But we must meet him halfway. We must try to cross the mountains ourselves," Ma said. The weather had turned sunny, though the air was bitterly cold. Perhaps Ma was right about leaving, even if she was wrong about Pa, Virginia thought. If Pa was not going to come for them, they must rescue themselves. They must leave before the snow started again.

"But Tommy and Jim are too little to cross the mountains, Ma Reed. They'll sink in the snow up to their necks," said Milt.

"I will ask the others to take them in until we can return for them. We still have a few hides left to trade. Patty will also have to stay behind, for I fear she is too weak to travel. You, Eliza, Milt and I will have to try to walk out of these mountains!" Ma was determined.

The Breens took in Tommy, Patty went to the Kesebergs, and the Graves took in Jim. Patty, especially, was despondent over being left behind.

"Are you sad because you have to stay with mean old Mr. Keseberg?" asked Virginia. Patty shook her head no. She simply did not want to be separated from her family.

"Mrs. Keseberg is sad because her baby died. Maybe I can make her feel better," said Patty. Virginia wished she could be more like Patty, thoughtful and considerate.

Virginia helped Patty pack her few things for her stay with the Kesebergs. Into Patty's pocket skirt went her doll, her constant companion now that Cash was gone. Since the death of her pet Cash, Patty had begun to talk to her doll, holding one-sided conversations with the tiny figure for hours. Virginia was afraid that, like Eliza, Patty was losing her mind from hunger. Into another pocket went a lock of Grandma Keyes' hair, given to Patty before her grandmother died.

"Grandma said that if I kept this, then I would always have her with me," said Patty.

"And what else do you have in that pocket skirt, Patty?" asked Virginia, remembering a time when all the pockets were filled, many of them with the sweets that Patty loved so well. It seemed so long ago that any of them had eaten a piece of candy.

"Just this," said Patty, as she pulled out a tiny crystal salt cellar that Virginia had last seen on the dining room table in their home in Springfield. That table had groaned with enough food each day that they had thrown some of it away at the end of each meal--juicy meat and fish, vegetables in rich sauces, fruit and cream pies, all fresh and delicious.

"And what will you do with this at the Kesebergs?" asked Virginia, taking the salt cellar that Patty held in her thin hand. They had run out of salt long ago.

"When we get to California, we'll need this salt cellar. I've carried it all this way," said Patty.

Virginia held the tiny crystal piece in the palm of her hand where it twinkled as if mocking her. Here they had no salt, nor anything to put the salt on. They had left so much behind and lost more along the way.

"If we get to California," said Virginia, handing the salt cellar back to Patty who tucked it away in her pocket skirt.

"You do the best you can to get over the mountain, Virginia. I'll do the best I can to make sure I and our brothers are here when you come for us," said Patty.

On January 4, Virginia, Milt, Eliza and Ma set off for the pass. Milt, because he was the heaviest, led them, trampling down the snow with his homemade oxbow snowshoes. Virginia, Ma and Eliza followed in his tracks. They took with them a little dried meat, a gift from the Breens who had had the most cattle to slaughter and preserve.

They trudged up the steep mountain all the first day and the struggle of climbing kept them from freezing in the bitter mountain air. That night, however, the wind picked up and the temperature dropped. Virginia heard the howling of some wild beast in the distance and she drew closer to Ma for comfort as much as warmth. They huddled around a fire built on top of the snow and as it burned, it melted a crater, with them in it. In the morning, they found themselves in a pool of icy water, and they had to climb out of the crater on their hands and knees.

"We'll all perish here, one way or another," said Eliza.

"We will not, Eliza. I will not watch any of my children, nor you and Milt either, die in these mountains. We are going to get across the pass and get help. Then we'll come back for the others," said Ma.

But Eliza shuddered and covered her face with her hands. "Mrs. Reed, If I'm going to die in these mountains, I'd rather die at the lake camp where folks'll bury my body.

Don't want to die in these mountains and have my body used as food for the wolves," Eliza sobbed.

Ma and Milt tried to reason with Eliza, to convince her that their best chance of survival was in moving forward, not in returning to camp. But Eliza would not be convinced even when Virginia begged her to remain with them.

In the morning, Eliza turned back to the camp. Virginia, Ma and Milt went forward. During the day, their constant movement kept their bodies warm, but the nights were bitterly cold and not even the campfire could warm them. Although they slept soundly, they awoke cold and hungry. On the third day, Virginia's feet became frostbitten, and she could not walk at all. Virginia scrambled over the snow drifts on her hands and knees, leaving a trail of blood in the snow, but no one noticed the crimson trail because the glare of the sunlight off the pure white snow had blinded the three travelers. And then they stopped climbing and began to descend. Finally they had reached the pass!

On the other side, Virginia collapsed in the snow and asked to rest. Milt picked Virginia up in his arms as though she were a baby. At first, she struggled and then she gave in to the numbness and leaned her weight against him. Milt carried Virginia for a short distance, but he was so weak and exhausted himself that he could not carry her far. And then he couldn't carry her at all.

"We must turn back," said Milt.

"You and Ma go on without me. It can't be far now. I'll wait here until you can send back help," said Virginia.

"We must all turn back," said Ma.

So close, they were so close to relief. They had already crossed the pass, and there was no guarantee that any of them would have the strength to return. Virginia was overcome with despair for the first time since their entrapment in these awful mountains. Eliza was right. They would all perish in this dreadful place.

They turned back. After four days and nights of traveling over the snow, they returned to the cabins by the lake. The very next day brought the fiercest snowstorm of the winter. Had they been caught in the open in such a storm, they would have surely died.

CHAPTER 12
Starvation Takes its Toll

"Virginia, you must take a little broth," said Ma, holding a spoonful of the glue pot stew to Virginia's lips. But Virginia was too exhausted to open her lips to receive it. If she refused food now, she wouldn't be obliged to suffer from hunger much longer, she thought. Pa was not coming for them after all, and so they had tried to rescue themselves. They had reached the summit but failed to descend to the valley below. What was there left, but to die as quickly as possible.

The Reeds were now staying with the Breens, since the Reeds' half of the cabin had no roof to keep out the snow and cold. Eliza was staying with the Graves who were also low on food, so Ma had given Eliza a piece of hide to boil into stew.

"It's all I have, Eliza, and you're welcome to it. It will keep you from starving until relief comes," said Ma.

"But Mrs. Reed, the spirits came to me in a vision. They told me not to eat the hide--it's unholy food! I'll die if I eat it!" said Eliza. Ma had sent Eliza back to the Graves to live or die on it.

Milt had taken shelter with the Murphys but he visited the Reeds every day, supplying them with firewood and buckets of snow to melt into drinking water. Fifteen people were crowded into the Breen cabin, and more than half of them, including the frostbitten Virginia, lay abed all day weak from hunger and cold. There was very little food left.

Even the Breens' pet, Towser, the last of the animals at the Lake camp, had gone into the stew pot.

"I shall give you what I can spare, but I've me own babes to think about ye know," said Peggy Breen. She gave Ma bones which had already been boiled twice, but Ma thanked her and boiled them for several days more until they turned to mush in the iron kettle. The result was tastier fare than the gluepot stew. The Reeds had eaten all but one of their hides.

"Should have started in eating the hides sooner and reserved some meat for later," said Mr. Breen to Ma when she asked for a bit of meat for the children. But they had not thought to be still in the mountains when the food ran out. They had believed Pa would come for them, bringing plenty of food to get them all safely over the pass to the valley below.

"Your Pa will come. He'll soon be here, with bread for you all," Ma assured her starving children. But Virginia no longer believed her.

"He's not coming. He thinks we're dead," said Virginia from her sick bed.

"You lose faith in your Pa and you lose faith in me," said Ma and Virginia was instantly sorry for her words. She would try to get better for Ma's sake. The next time Ma offered a spoonful of broth, she swallowed it.

When her husband wasn't looking, sometimes the good-hearted Peggy Breen slipped a few pieces of meat between Virginia's lips, for Mrs. Breen had always liked the plucky girl who was the friend of her firstborn son. Soon, Virginia began to gather a little of her old strength. Sometimes in the evenings, John Breen would sit by her bed and read to her from one of two books the Breens had found in the cabin. The first was *The Life of Daniel Boone.* Virginia enjoyed hearing about other people who survived in the wilderness, enduring hardship and deprivation as they were. The other book was the Bible. All the Breens took great interest in the stories of the Bible. The words from the book of Job exploded in Virginia's head as John's smooth voice read to her. Virginia cried out for God to have mercy on Job, on her, on all of them.

Each evening, the Breens kneeled down on the hard dirt floor of the crowded cabin. Mr. Breen, holding a lighted stick in place of a candle, then led his family in prayer, always ending with a plea for God to send them relief soon if He should see fit. Ma and the Reed children held their own silent prayer sessions as they had always done. They asked for much the same as the Breens.

One night after everyone had gone to bed, Virginia could not sleep. She rose from her sick bed and knelt on the cabin floor and clasped her hands as she had seen the Breens do.

She had put her faith in Pa and then in herself, but relief had not come. Now she would put her faith in God. "Dear God, if you send us relief and let me see my father again, I shall become a Catholic," she said aloud. The others in the crowded cabin did not stir. Virginia wondered if the time was not too far distant when they should all be asleep forever.

As starvation took its toll, some of the weakest began to die. Mrs. Keseberg's baby, Lewis, was already dead. So was Landrum Murphy. Then Mrs. Eddy and her baby died within minutes of each other. They had not heard from the Donner families at Aldar Creek for weeks. The snows were too deep and the people too weak to make the six-mile hike.

When dear Milt died on February 10, Virginia and Ma dragged his body out of the Graves cabin and covered him with snow. Virginia cried when she gazed down at his gaunt face for the last time. He had been like a brother to her, carrying her over the snow when she could not walk. And he had been like a son to Ma, never leaving the Reed family after Pa's banishment. Virginia covered Milt's face, patting the pure white snow over his beloved features, and she wept.

"Milt loved you too. He looked up to you Virginia, even though you were so much younger," said Ma, putting her arms around her daughter and pulling her close.

No matter how much Virginia understood hunger and hardship, she had never understood the people she loved. How wrong Virginia had been about Milt, and about so many of those she thought she had known so well when they first started their trip west. Milt, she had thought slow and stupid, always waiting to take direction from someone else. But he had shown himself to be better than smart. He had been loyal to the Reed family to the very end.

And Virginia had been wrong about Eliza, too. She had thought Eliza courageous and brave. Eliza had laughed and told funny stories when the rest of them were nervous or anxious about what lay ahead. Eliza had not been afraid even of the Indians on the plains. Now Eliza lay in the Graves cabin, her spirit broken and her mind crazed by hunger because she refused to eat the glue pot stew that might sustain her.

She had been wrong about Patty, too. Just because Patty was quiet and thoughtful didn't mean Patty didn't have hopes and dreams as strong and powerful as her own. Virginia thought about the tiny salt cellar that Patty had carried all the way from Illinois, keeping it always with her though it had long ago ceased to be useful. Virginia would have thrown away the salt cellar in order to forget what she could not have, but Patty had held on to it as a reminder of what she would soon have again.

But most of all, Virginia had been wrong about Ma. Virginia had thought Ma as delicate as the china cups from which Ma sipped her tea back in Springfield. But Ma was as strong as the tall pines that towered over them in camp. Like the pines, Ma's love had provided the shelter and warmth that had held her family together since Pa had left. Ma had not been too ladylike to bargain and beg when necessary to make sure her children and hired help had something to eat. And Ma had shown the rest of them how to be strong even when they felt like giving up. Ma's belief that her beloved husband would return for his family had never been shaken even though Virginia's own trust in her father had faltered.

True to her word to Pa, Ma did not shed a tear since her husband's banishment. Ma did not cry now. Not even for Milt. Virginia and Ma said a prayer over Milt's snowy grave. Then, together, they went to the Murphy cabin to retrieve what few possessions Milt still had: his tools, firearms, a few blankets, and the one remaining hide from the Reed cabin roof.

"I'll take the hide in return for sheltering Milt," said the pale, gaunt Mrs. Murphy. Her eyes were ringed with dark circles and her sunken cheeks gave her the appearance of death.

"This is the last of my hides, Lavina," said Ma. You can take the gun--it'll be useful for hunting game. But I need to boil the hide to feed my children," said Ma.

"We don't have anything to feed the children in this cabin. If we can't eat the hide, maybe we'll commence on Milt," said Mrs. Murphy.

Later, Virginia would wonder why it took her so long to realize what was happening on the shores of Truckee Lake.

CHAPTER 13
The Reunion

One evening, Virginia and John Breen and Patty were sitting on a blanket outside the stuffy, windowless cabin. From out of the pines stepped an Indian. He had a small pack on his back and he was wrapped in a fur blanket. The children sat motionless as he approached, not daring to believe their eyes. The Indian spoke to them, but they did not understand his words and they kept silent, too weak to be afraid.

The Indian took off his pack and rummaged around inside it, pulled out a root that looked somewhat like a potato. He held it out to John, who took it. The Indian gave a root to Patty and another to Virginia, and then the Indian put his pack back on his back and walked off into the pines.

"Was he real or did we see a mirage?" Patty asked, but in their hands they held the roots that the Indian gave them, so he must have been real.

"What did he say?" asked John. No one had understood his language, but the important thing was that he had spoken to them. Someone, at least, knew that they were here and that they were hungry!

On February 18, Virginia awoke to the sound of an unfamiliar voice.

"Halloo! Anybody here?"

Slowly, the others in the cabin began to stir from their sleep. They sat up and looked at each other, puzzled at the sound of the stranger's voice, but too weak to move quickly. Finally, Peggy Breen stood and went to the cabin door. She opened the door and climbed up out of the snow.

"Are you men from California? Or do you come from heaven?" asked Mrs. Breen, her voice thin and hollow.

And then Virginia heard the sound of familiar voices from the other cabins.

"Relief! Relief!"

Thank God! The rescuers had found them at last.

Soon, all that were able had emptied the cabins to greet their seven rescuers.

"Did you bring food?" was the question on everyone's lips. The rescuers quickly distributed food from their packs--bread, jerked venison, dried fruit.

"Eat slowly and in small amounts," cautioned Mr. Glover, the leader of the rescue party. Virginia put a small piece of the dried apple into her mouth and was delighted at the strange sweetness of it. How long had it been since she had tasted fruit? Five months at least.

"We sent out a rescue party on snowshoes weeks ago, led by Charles Stanton. Why aren't they with you?" asked Mr. Breen.

"Stanton died in the snow. Only a few of the snowshoers made it through to tell us of your plight. Their feet were too frostbitten for them to return with us," he said.

"And what of James Reed? Have you heard of him?" asked Ma.

"Reed's not more than three days behind us," he answered. Ma swayed slightly and then reached out for

Virginia who held her tightly. Pa was coming! He hadn't forgotten them! He was coming for them!

The next day, some of the rescuers hiked to the Donner camp and returned with six of the refugees, including Uncle George and Tamsen's daughter, 12-year-old Leanna. The news was bad.

"Pa's dying from the infection in his hand. Ma won't leave him, and Aunt Betsy and the younger ones are weak from hunger. There's nothing left to eat," said Leanna.

Mr. Glover, the head of the rescue party told them that as many as possible would have to leave the camps on foot the following day. They would leave all of their available food behind for those in camp, which should last them until the second rescue party arrived. The rescuers had cached food along their route to feed themselves and all those who could walk with them out of the mountains.

"We should stay here and wait for Pa," said Virginia.

"Most likely you'll meet your Pa on the way out," assured Mr. Glover. The Reeds would have to go. They had no food left at all.

Virginia said goodbye to her friend, John Breen, who decided to stay behind with most of his family to wait the second rescue party. The Breens still had enough food left to survive the wait.

On February 22, 23 people, including the entire Reed family, prepared to walk out of the mountains. They left the cabins and entered the pine forest walking single file in the tracks of the rescuers' snowshoes. As she trudged along through the snow towards the pass for the second time,

Virginia remembered not to watch the snow, which in its pristine brightness could cause one to go blind. Ma walked ahead of her, and Patty and her two little brothers trudged along behind her. Three year old Tommy quickly grew tired, but he struggled on without complaint, climbing over the hills of snow between each track of the snowshoe. His little legs were too short to allow him to walk from one step to another.

"You can do it, Tommy. Take another step just like the last one. Remember, each step you take gets you closer to Pa," said Virginia. She grabbed his arm and helped him over the next mound of snow.

Patty was also struggling. Although she had never once complained, she had seemed to suffer the most from the lack of food. Now, at the end of the first day's march, Patty's famine ravaged body was giving out and she fell into the snow, exhausted. Ma encouraged her to get up, but Patty could not. By evening, the Reeds had fallen far behind the others.

"You'll have to send Patty and Tommy back to camp to wait for the next rescue party, Mrs. Reed. They aren't strong enough for the crossing," said Mr. Glover.

"I've kept my family together all this time and I guess I'll not be parting with them now," said Ma, defiant.

"Stragglers jeopardize the lives of all your children, as well as all of us, Mrs. Reed. They must go back. One of my men will take them back to the Breens," said Mr. Glover.

"Mr. Glover, you must promise me on your honor that if the second relief party doesn't get through, you will return yourself to rescue my children," said Ma.

"On my honor, I promise you that, Mrs. Reed," he said.

Ma and Virginia hugged Patty and Tommy. Jim cried. Though Virginia tried not to cry, she feared she would never see her brother and sister again. Most of those back at the camps were starving, and those trying to get out of the mountains might never make it in their weakened conditions. But Patty was brave.

"If you never see me again, do the best you can," she told Ma. Then Patty took little Tommy's hand and began the struggle back to the cabins by the lake. Virginia and Ma and Jim watched as they disappeared into the trees. Virginia and Jim wept, but Ma was dry eyed.

They moved on, climbing ever upward. At night they slept in their clothes near the fire, which melted the snow that clung to their pants and skirts, leaving them wet and uncomfortable. When the fire burned out in the hours before daylight, their wet clothes froze stiff, making it difficult to move.

Finally, they crossed the mountain pass, but they were still not out of the mountains. Wild animals had dug up the food supply that the rescuers had so carefully cached for the return trip, and once again they were facing starvation. Mr. Glover rationed a small piece of meat and two teaspoons full of flour daily to each of them. How much longer before they reached the sunny California valley, wondered Virginia. And where was Pa and the second rescue party they had hoped to meet on the trail?

On their sixth day in the mountains, as they struggle through the snowdrifts, Virginia was startled to hear a familiar voice call from out of the forest. Several men stepped out of the trees ahead of them.

"Is Mrs. Reed with you? Tell her Mr. Reed is here." Beside Virginia, Ma dropped to her knees in the snow.

"It's Pa," shouted Jim, and he ran forward to greet his father.

Virginia ran a few steps in the snow to meet Pa, but fell down. She crawled forward on her hands and knees. And then she was folded in Pa's arms and he held on to her tightly.

"Your mother, my child, where is she?" asked Pa. Virginia pointed to where Ma still knelt in the snow. Although Ma was laughing, tears were running down her face. Ma was crying tears of joy.

That night, Pa baked bread for them in the ashes of their campfire.

"I wasn't wrong about California, Margaret," said Pa, when they were all gathered together. "Green grass, horses to ride, plenty to eat."

Virginia closed her eyes and tried to envision these things. It had seemed ages since she had seen bare ground or ridden a horse or had enough to eat.

"And tomorrow, you will reach Bear Valley and you will have these things," said Pa. "Tomorrow, I will leave you one more time--I must get Patty and Tommy out of those mountains." Ma reached out and took Pa's gloved hand in her own. She did not say "don't go."

The next morning, they said goodbye to Pa. They watched him and the other men in the relief party until they were out of sight and then they continued their way down the mountains. They could see the green valley below them and a river sparkled blue in the sunlight. Virginia looked behind her, up at the steep face of the mountain cliffs, at the snowy pass they had finally crossed. She had just finished the most dangerous part of the journey, but Pa was just starting it.

On March 4 they reached Sutter's Fort, where they were taken in with Mrs. Sinclair, who gave them clean clothes and plenty to eat. For the first time since leaving Illinois, Virginia would sleep in a real bed, with clean sheets and warm dry blankets. A cheerful fire blazed in the stone fireplace of her bedroom. But that night Virginia found that she could not sleep, and she crawled out of bed and stood at the window staring out into the darkness. Beyond the foothills just behind the veil of darkness rose the Sierra Nevada. And although she could not see it in the murky darkness, high at the top of the snowy peaks was the rocky pass she had crossed just a few days before. As Virginia stood there, staring off in the direction of the mountains, a light rain began to beat against the window glass. Virginia shivered and hugged her thin body clad in the scented cotton nightgown that Mrs. Sinclair had given her. If there was rain in the valley, there would be snow in the mountains.

AFTERWARD

Extreme hunger and deprivation led to desperate acts among those caught in the snows of the Sierra Nevada in the winter of 1846-47. When James Reed and the second rescue party arrived at the Murphy cabin, they found evidence of cannibalism--Mrs. Murphy had indeed "commenced on Milt" and eaten him. Further evidence of cannibalism was found at the Donner tents. Virginia Reed wrote in a letter to her cousin a few weeks after her rescue "but thank God we have all got through and the only family that did not eat human flesh". But the Reeds may have not been the "only" family. The Breens, who were the best supplied with food at the outset and began rationing earlier than the others, probably did not eat human flesh either.

The most atrocious incidents of cannibalism occurred amongst those of the Donner Party who had left the Truckee Lake camps on snowshoes in December. As Virginia was not with this group, I did not include the story of the snowshoers' ordeal within *One Eternal Winter*. Not only did members of the snowshoers group cannibalize the bodies of their comrades who gave out and died, they plotted and carried out the murders of the two Indian guides and then roasted and consumed their flesh.

Unfortunately, the term "cannibals" has been firmly associated with the members of the Donner Party to the exclusion of other incidents which show a brighter side of the human condition. Extremity can bring out the worst in the human character, but there is ample evidence in the story of the Donner Party that extremity can also be a catalyst for courage and faith of heroic proportions.

Throughout the diaries and writings of the Donner Party members, one can read of the supreme sacrifices made for the welfare of others. Stanton's willingness to return with supplies to the struggling wagon train even though he had no family amongst the emigrants to relieve is one example. Milt's loyalty to the Reed family when he might have been better off fending for himself is another. Margaret Reed's source of strength to save her children regardless of the cost to herself is a quality that might not have surfaced in the aristocratic life she led in Illinois. As Tamsen Donner noted in a letter to her sister, "We have some of the best people in our company and some, too, that are not so good."

While for some, extreme suffering seemed to spawn despair and hopelessness, even insanity, others never gave up hope. When Patty Reed arrived in California, she pulled from the pockets of her apron three things--a lock of her grandmother's hair, a tiny salt shaker, and her doll--tangible symbols of her will to live. The doll is on display at Sutter's Fort State Historic Park in Sacramento.

Virginia, on the other hand, seemed to draw her strength from a combination of inner resources not represented by tangible things-- intense love of family, confidence in her own ability to survive, and faith in God--resources that helped her to struggle and endure one eternal winter.

Note: On March 3, James Reed led Patty and Tommy and fifteen others out of camp toward the pass. Those left behind were too weak or sick to travel and would await a third relief party.

All of the Donner adults died in the mountain camps. The Graves children were orphaned and Mr. Eddy lost his entire family. The Kesebergs lost both their children. Only the Reeds and the Breens suffered no loss of life.

After their rescue, the Reed family members were reunited and settled in San Jose, where James Reed made his fortune in real estate speculation. James and Margaret adopted two of the orphaned Donner children and had two more children of their own. Margaret's sick headaches disappeared.

Virginia Reed eloped with John Murphy two years after she reached California. They had nine children. Ironically, her husband had helped to build the cabin used by the Breens and the Reeds during their mountain ordeal. He was not related to the Murphy family that was part of the Donner party, however. During her lifetime, Virginia became an accomplished equestrian and competed at county fairs. She kept the vow she had made during her illness in the mountains, and converted to Roman Catholicism, much to her father's dismay. Virginia Reed Murphy died at age 87.

Patty Reed married Frank Lewis at age 18 and had eight children. John and Edward Breen became prosperous ranchers. Eliza Williams recovered quickly and regained enough weight to be described as portly. She married soon after her arrival in California.

ILLUSTRATIONS

Virginia Reed

Virginia Reed survived the ordeal of the winter of 1846-47. She grew up, married at age 14, and wrote her remembrance of the events of that awful winter in an article published in *New Century Magazine*, July 1891. Source: C. F. McGlashan, *History of the Donner Party*.

Not one of the Reed family perished during the terrible winter they were trapped in the Sierra Nevada. Patty Reed's doll, shown here, is on display at the Sutter's Fort Historical Park. Courtesy California Department of Parks and Recreation.

Once known as Truckee Lake, this body of water is now known as Donner Lake in memory of the emigrants who made their tragic winter camp near its frozen shores. In this view, the author looks out over the lake toward the snow capped Donner Pass. Photo by Jane Ann Turzillo.

The Truckee River follows the main emigrant trail into California. The first emigrants to discover the Truckee basin were the Stephen-Townsend-Murphy Party, which passed through in 1844. Photo by the author.

In January 1847, a few of the ill-fated Donner Party were able to climb up and over the 7,088-foot pass, now known as the Donner Pass. Photo by the author.

Several severe storms swept through the Truckee basin during the winter of 1846-47. Even in the late spring, the weather can be fierce and unpredictable. This photograph was taken in June. Photo by the author.

A museum and memorial are now located at the main Donner Party campsite. This tablet marks the location of the Graves cabin. Virginia spent part of the winter at this spot, located beside the present day Donner Pass Road (Old U.S. 40). Photo by Jane Ann Turzillo.

Several miles from the main camp was Alder Creek, the campsite of the Donner families. Some members of the family spent the winter in this crude shelter made of branches covered with animal hides. Photo by Jane Ann Turzillo.

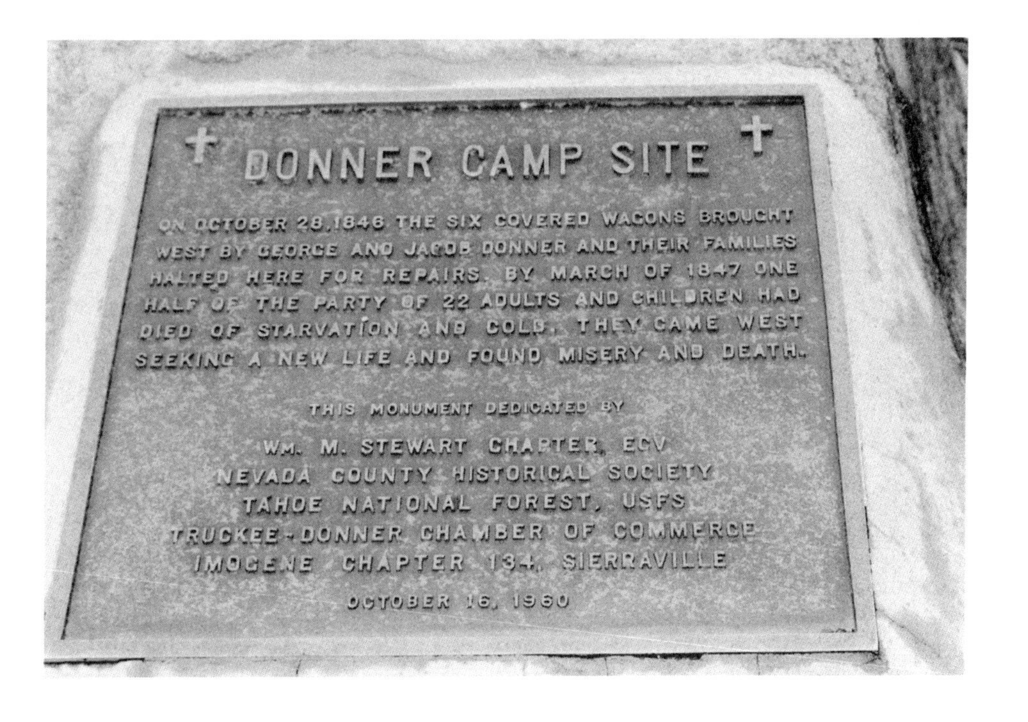

All of the Donner adults died during the winter of 1846-47. This plaque marks the Donner campsite at Alder Creek. Photo by Jane Ann Turzillo.

The face of this rock formed the north end and the fireplace of the Murphy cabin. According to the inscription, General Stephen W. Kearny, on June 22, 1847, buried under the middle of the cabin the bodies found in the vicinity. Photo by Jane Ann Turzillo.

A close-up of the Murphy cabin plaque shows a complete list of the members of the Donner Party. Photo by Jane Ann Turzillo.

Donner Memorial State Park is now located near where Virginia and her family spent the terrible winter of 1846-47. This Pioneer Monument was erected to memorialize the brave men, women and children who journeyed westward seeking a better way of life. The monument base is 22 feet high, the same height as the snow in the winter of 1846-47. The bronze tablet reads: *Virile to risk and find; kindly withal and a ready help. Facing the brunt of fate: Indomitable--unafraid.* Photo by Jane Ann Turzillo.

BIBLIOGRAPHY

Across the Plains in the Donner Party: A Personal Narrative of the Overland Trip to California, 1846-1847, by Virginia Reed Murphy, Century Magazine, July 1891.

The Donner Party, a documentary film written and directed by Ric Burns, Direct Cinema Limited, 1992.

Lovina's Song, A Pioneer Girl's Journey With the Donner Party, by Marian Rudolph, Citron Bay Press, 1999.

Ordeal by Hunger: The Story of the Donner Party, by George R. Stewart, Houghton Mifflin Company, 1936.

Patty Reed's Doll, by Rachel Laurgaard, Tomato Enterprises, 1989. (juvenile fiction)

The Perilous Journey of the Donner Party, by Marian Calabro, Clarion Books, 1999. (juvenile nonfiction)

Pioneer Children on the Journey West, by Emmy E. Werner, Westview Press, 1995.

Snowbound: The Tragic Story of the Donner Party, by David Lavender, Holiday House, 1996. (juvenile nonfiction)

In addition, the following site compiled by Dan M. Rosen includes daily logs, diary entries, trail location, maps, photos and drawings of the Donner Party trip: *http://members.aol.com/DanMRosen/donner/index.htm*